Showtime

Oprah Winfrey started as the host of *A.M. Chicago* on January 2, 1984. A curly-haired woman in a big fur coat, she introduced herself outside the WLS-TV studios with the University of Illinois marching band blaring out a welcome behind her. Chicago had little time to ask itself, "What's an Oprah?" She took the city by storm, and within a month, almost everyone in the city knew who she was.

Oprah had auditioned for the job in the fall of 1983. Station manager Dennis Swanson had her sit in front of a camera and chat about herself and her interests. After she was finished, Oprah met with Swanson in his office. Even though he was delighted with her audition, he felt that he couldn't totally show his enthusiasm. After all, he was going to have to negotiate a salary with her as soon as he offered her the job.

"How do you think it went?" Oprah asked.

"I think it went pretty well," he replied. But he was thinking that Oprah's was the greatest audition tape he had ever seen.

READ ALL THE BOOKS IN THE
UP*close* SERIES

UPclose:

Oprah Winfrey

a twentieth-century life by
ILENE COOPER

PUFFIN BOOKS

PUFFIN BOOKS
Published by the Penguin Group
Penguin Young Readers Group, 345 Hudson Street, New York, New York 10014, U.S.A.
Penguin Group (Canada), 90 Eglinton Avenue East, Suite 700, Toronto, Ontario, Canada M4P 2Y3
(a division of Pearson Penguin Canada Inc.)
Penguin Books Ltd, 80 Strand, London WC2R 0RL, England
Penguin Ireland, 25 St Stephen's Green, Dublin 2, Ireland (a division of Penguin Books Ltd)
Penguin Group (Australia), 250 Camberwell Road, Camberwell, Victoria 3124, Australia
(a division of Pearson Australia Group Pty Ltd)
Penguin Books India Pvt Ltd, 11 Community Centre, Panchsheel Park, New Delhi - 110 017, India
Penguin Group (NZ), 67 Apollo Drive, Rosedale, North Shore 0632, New Zealand
(a division of Pearson New Zealand Ltd)
Penguin Books (South Africa) (Pty) Ltd, 24 Sturdee Avenue, Rosebank, Johannesburg 2196, South Africa

Registered Offices: Penguin Books Ltd, 80 Strand, London WC2R 0RL, England

First published in the United States of America by Viking, a division of Penguin Young Readers Group, 2007
Published by Puffin Books, a division of Penguin Young Readers Group, 2008

10 9 8 7 6 5 4 3 2 1

Photo credits can be found on page 207.

LIBRARY OF CONGRESS CATALOGING-IN-PUBLICATION DATA IS AVAILABLE

Puffin Books ISBN 978-0-14-241045-5

Set in Goudy
Book design by Jim Hoover

Printed in the United States of America

For Iva Freeman   —I.C.

Best Wish

Ihn Corr

2008 .

UPclose:

Oprah Winfrey

Contents

Foreword

WHEN I WAS ASKED by Viking Children's Books to do a biography for their new Up Close series, the editor wondered if I would be interested in writing about Oprah Winfrey. "You've come to the right place," I assured her. As a lifelong Chicagoan, I remember very well when Oprah arrived in Chicago in 1984 to host a local talk show, A.M. *Chicago*. It is no overstatement to say she took the town by storm.

How and why exactly that happened is explored in this biography. Certainly there was an element of novelty involved. Yet it was not just that Oprah Winfrey was an African American in a medium that was mostly white, or that she was a plus-size woman in a business where thinness is prized. Oprah has a rare and special talent—an ability to communicate with her audience so intimately that it makes her seem more like a friend than a broadcaster. Chicago had never seen anyone quite like Oprah Winfrey, and people across the country and throughout the world felt the same once her show became nationally and then globally syndicated.

Over the more than twenty years that Oprah Winfrey has been in Chicago, she and her show have evolved, both becoming ever more influential. Though now an international celebrity, Oprah began as a local star, and I feel as if I've had a ringside seat watching her rise into the stratosphere. Yet as I've come to know her better while writing this book, what I ultimately admire most about Oprah is her commitment to doing good. This quality has inspired millions of people throughout the world to get involved, to think about others, and to find ways to solve problems. As Oprah herself has said, "The happiness you feel is in direct proportion to the love you are able to give." It is this message I hope readers take away from Oprah's story.

Introduction

OPRAH WINFREY WAS being given another chance. In 1976, only twenty-two years old, she had been hired to be a newscaster in Baltimore on WJZ-TV. But things hadn't worked out very well. The station had paired her up with an older, well-established broadcaster who didn't want a coanchor at all, and certainly not a young black woman whose TV experience had come in the small TV market of Nashville.

The mismatch showed on the air. To make things worse, the station management was having big doubts about Oprah herself. They didn't appreciate her casual speaking style, so different from the formality broadcasters showed on a nightly news show. Nor did her bosses like the way she looked. They suggested changes in her appearance with sometimes disastrous results—like the time they wanted her hair straightened, and it all fell out!

Soon Oprah was removed from her anchor chair and sent out to be a street reporter, frequently covering murders and natural disasters. Those assignments didn't work out either. Oprah hated having to shove a microphone in the face of someone who had just suffered a tragedy.

Oprah Winfrey could see the writing on the wall. Surely, she was about to be fired. Then something unexpected happened. WJZ-TV was planning a new program, an interview show called *People Are Talking*, and Oprah was named the cohost. Wearing a pretty pink dress and flashing a big smile, she eagerly started her new assignment. By the time the first show was over, she realized the immediate impact it had made on her life.

"I came off of that stage August 14, 1978, and I knew that I was home. In all my years of being discontent, feeling like something's not quite right, feeling like I was in the wrong place, in the wrong job, I knew this is it. It felt like home because it felt so natural. It felt like I could be myself."

Oprah Winfrey was now a talk-show host, and the world of television would never quite be the same again.

One

IT WAS A COLD day on a lonesome Mississippi farm. Four-year-old Oprah Winfrey sat on the back porch, churning up some butter for the family table and watching as her grandmother poked at clothes floating in an old black pot. Wooden clothespins decorated Grandma Hattie Mae Lee's apron. As she lifted the heavy, wet laundry out of the water and hung each piece on the line, Hattie told her granddaughter, "Pay attention now. You're going to have to learn to do this someday."

Oprah didn't answer. But a voice inside her head said plainly, *No, Grandma, I won't.*

There was no reason for Oprah Winfrey to think that she wouldn't have to earn her living taking in laundry like her grandmother, or cleaning houses like her mother, who lived up north. Born on January 29, 1954, Oprah was the great-great-granddaughter of slaves, and in Mississippi, where she was growing up, segregation still shaped and bent the lives of African Americans.

Her family life was unsettled as well. Oprah lived with her grandparents, Hattie and Earlist Lee. Hattie was loving but strict. Earlist was a frightening figure who would throw things at Oprah or shoo her away with his cane. Oprah's parents weren't married; they barely knew each other. As an adult, Oprah said that her birth was "the result of a one-day fling under an oak tree." Her father, Vernon Winfrey, a twenty-year-old soldier stationed at Fort Rucker, Alabama, didn't even know he had a baby until he received a newspaper clipping announcing the birth. Her mother Vernita, eighteen, attached a curt note that said, "Send clothes."

Life didn't start out easy for Oprah, an illegitimate child born poor and black, and harder times were to come. Yet even as a child, she never saw her future as limited in any way. Oprah has said as she looks back to those early days, listening to her elders talk about the hardships they endured, "I never believed that would be my life. I believed I belonged to someone or something bigger than myself, my family, even Mississippi. I believed I was God's child. Therefore, I could do anything."

Not many people can say they have a name that no one else does. But it's a fair bet that baby Winfrey was the first Oprah. Her great-aunt Ida was given the honor of naming her. A churchgoing woman, Aunt Ida decided that she would name the baby after the biblical Orpah, from the Old Testament's Book of Ruth. But folks misheard the name and started calling the infant Oprah. It stuck.

The town where Oprah Winfrey was born has an unusual name, too: Kosciusko. Seventy miles north of Mississippi's capital of Jackson, set between the Big Black and Pearl Rivers, it takes its name from Thaddeus Kosciuszko, a Polish general who fought in the American Revolution. Kosciuszko was so passionately opposed to the soul-killing practice of slavery that had taken hold in the fledgling country, he left money in his will to buy the freedom of Thomas Jefferson's slaves. There is an irony in the fact that the town named for him was in the deepest South, where life for black people was difficult at best—and tragic at worst—both before and after the Civil War.

Oprah lived outside of Kosciusko in a rickety old farmhouse so basic, there was no indoor plumbing. To get there from town, visitors had to come up a dusty, unpaved road, and once they arrived, there wasn't much to see. It was just a small farm with a few animals and

This sign marks the spot in Kosciusko, Mississippi, where Oprah Winfrey spent the first six years of her life (the house has been demolished). Although the sign calls Oprah's parents Mr. and Mrs. Vernon Winfrey, they were never married.

never-ending chores. Even a little girl like Oprah had to help, so she fed the hogs and took the cows out to pasture. The water she drew from the well was used for drinking and washing. There was plenty to eat, all of it grown on the farm, but money was in short supply, so there were few modern conveniences. No telephone. No television. "I never had a store-bought dress," Oprah remembered later.

And it was lonely. The nearest neighbor was an elderly blind man—one night Hattie had to scream for him when Earlist loomed menacingly over the bed where Hattie and Oprah slept. As for children, none lived nearby, so Oprah talked to the animals—the cattle, chickens, and hogs—and told them stories. Her one toy was a doll that Hattie had fashioned from a corncob.

As an adult, Oprah didn't remember that her mother had lived with her on the farm at all. It seemed as if she had always been gone. Actually Vernita stayed on the farm until Oprah was about four, but after the local cotton mills shut down, there was no longer any way for her to earn a living. "I wanted to leave Mississippi, so I could get a job and take care of her," Vernita remembered later. Like thousands of other African

Americans before her, Vernita was part of a steady stream of people who decided to move north, where there were jobs and possibilities. Vernita's brothers had already moved to Chicago, so that was her first stop. But she liked nearby Milwaukee better, so she settled there.

With her mother gone, the only woman who counted in Oprah's life was her grandmother, and Hattie Mae was a powerful figure. A no-nonsense woman, Mama, as Oprah called her, was teacher, protector, and disciplinarian. She was not a woman who tolerated fools, and she was determined that her granddaughter was going to use all the gifts and talents that she had. Although Hattie had minimal formal education herself, she had a great respect for learning. When Oprah was only a small child, Hattie taught her to read, and as an adult Oprah realized the importance of that simple yet profound effort: "My grandmother taught me to read, and that opened all kinds of possibilities for me." Many times, Oprah has called reading the foundation for her success.

Oprah used this new skill well. By age three, she was memorizing and performing dramatic readings in church. Hattie was a regular attendant at the Faith United Mississippi Baptist Church, and Oprah always went with her. Church could be boring, especially during the hot, humid summers, when the little girl would gaze up at the achingly slow ceiling fan pushing around the heavy air. But now, she was a star. The preacher would call her up to the front of the congregation, saying, "Little Mistress Winfrey will render a recitation." The first one she gave was on Easter: "Jesus rose on Easter day. Hallelujah. Hallelujah, and the angels did proclaim." A pigtailed girl, her hair full of barrettes, wearing her Easter dress and new patent-leather shoes, Oprah immediately took to being in the spotlight and spoke in church often.

"Hattie Mae, that girl is gifted," the ladies of the church would say, nodding and fanning themselves with paper fans.

For Oprah, public speaking was a way to get attention and love. It felt good to make her grandmother proud. Yet as pleased as Hattie Mae was with Oprah's accomplishments, she never hesitated to punish her when she felt it was necessary—and in Oprah's memory, Hattie Mae felt like it was necessary a lot. The punishment was a whipping—or a "whuppin'," as her grandmother called it. When she misbehaved, Oprah was told to go outside and get a switch—a tree branch—that Hattie Mae would use to hit her. As an adult, Oprah remembered the harshness of the beatings. "She could whip me for days and days and never get tired. It would be called child abuse now."

Back then, it just seemed like the way of the world. There seems to be no doubt that, despite the severity of her girlhood punishments, the adult Oprah remembers equally clearly the affection and gifts of learning and faith that Hattie Mae bestowed on her. "Some of my most comforting memories," she has said, "are of sitting between my grandmother's skirted knees, while she scratched my head and oiled my scalp. It was our ritual, one we performed again and again, right there on the front porch—as did many a black girl growing up in the South. Today I know enough to know that the comfort was about all I was getting out of our little ritual, because it wasn't doing my hair a bit of good. But it felt great at the time."

She also felt close to her grandmother when the two were sharing a prayer on bended knees before they went to bed, or when they talked about God. Hattie Mae wanted Oprah to trust God, but sometimes that was hard for the girl. Oprah remembers the time she started crying because she realized that someday she was going to die.

"Honey," Hattie Mae comforted her, "God doesn't mess with his children. You gotta do a lot of work in your life and not be afraid. The strong have got to take care of the others."

As Oprah got a little older, she realized that her grandmother was loosely quoting from a part of the New Testament (Romans 15:1) that talked about people taking care of one another. "Despite my age," Oprah has said, "I somehow grasped the concept. I knew I was going to help people. That I had a higher calling, so to speak." As far as she is concerned, her success is built around the strong center of faith, hard work, and hope that her grandmother instilled in her. "I am where I am because of my grandmother. My strength. My sense of reasoning. Everything. All of that was set by the time I was six years old. I am basically no different now than when I was six."

When children are young, they often think things

will always stay the same. Oprah's life in Mississippi had a reassuring consistency: church and chores, reading and recitations. Then, suddenly and startlingly, everything changed. By 1959, Vernita had gotten herself settled in Milwaukee and she wanted her daughter living there with her. Hattie Mae, whose husband had recently died, was getting older and feeling poorly. She was ready to let Oprah go.

Farm life was over. There would be no more quiet, lonely days telling stories to animals. No more time to spend with her fierce but loving grandmother. Oprah was moving north to a big noisy city full of lights, motion, and people. Changes and surprises awaited her. Not all of them would be pleasant.

Two

SIX-YEAR-OLD OPRAH WINFREY must have felt a little like Alice stepping through the looking glass when she arrived in Milwaukee, Wisconsin, a bustling city ninety miles north of Chicago. Everything was different from what she had known. The winters were freezing, the pace of life was quick, and the noise of the city—horns honking, radios blaring, trucks lumbering through the streets—could be overwhelming.

All the things that she had taken for granted in her young life had disappeared in the space of time it took to drive the 750 miles between Mississippi and Milwaukee. Life on the farm may have been lonely, but at least there was room to roam on the family's several acres, and Oprah could play among the land's fragrant pines. In Milwaukee, all Oprah's mother,

Vernita, could afford in the way of living quarters was a dingy room in a boardinghouse. Instead of being raised by a grandmother with a watchful eye, Oprah was often left to her own devices while Vernita was away cleaning houses in the Milwaukee suburbs. And where once Oprah spent the day communing with the cows and practicing her recitations for the chickens, now her only pets were the cockroaches that scurried around the boardinghouse. "You'd find a whole family of them," Oprah remembered as an adult. "I would name them and put them in a jar and feed them . . . like kids catching lightning bugs. I named two of them Melinda and Sandy."

But the biggest surprise waiting for Oprah in Milwaukee was her new baby sister. The unmarried Vernita had once again gotten pregnant, and the result was little Patricia, whom Oprah was expected to help care for. Oprah had mixed feelings about Patricia. She was a cute baby and more fun to play with than a corncob doll, but it was difficult to share Vernita's limited time and attention—especially with a sister who seemed to be her mother's favorite. Patricia was lighter-skinned than Oprah, a feature that was often preferred in the black community.

Milwaukee was a bustling city when Oprah Winfrey moved there in 1960.
This photo shows the busy downtown around the time she arrived.

Oprah was aware of her looks even as a little girl back in Mississippi. She remembers sleeping with a clothespin on her nose (with two bits of cotton on either side to buffer the pain) because she wanted to look like the child star Shirley Temple. Now she felt like she was being shunted aside because her sister was considered prettier. Vernita and Patricia slept inside, but the woman who owned the boardinghouse made Oprah sleep in an enclosed porch.

If all of this wasn't unsettling enough, Oprah was soon to learn that the things she had been most prized for in Mississippi—her love of reading and her public-speaking abilities—were not held in very high esteem by her mother. Oprah still remembers how shocked she was when her mother found her reading and pulled the book out of her hands. "You're nothing but a book-worm," Vernita told her. "You think you're better than the other kids."

It must have been confusing for young Oprah. Although her grandmother had hardly been lavish with compliments, Oprah had seen how pleased Hattie was when the churchgoers praised her granddaughter as "gifted." Oprah herself had heard that comment often enough that she says she started to believe it. "I didn't even know what gifted meant, but I just thought it meant I was somebody special." Hugging that feeling close to her is what kept her going in the harder times that would come. Young Oprah wasn't about to let anybody spoil that feeling for her, including her mother, and even Vernita was grudgingly impressed with how much confidence the girl had in herself. Vernita remembers how at age eight, Oprah told her, "'I'm going to fly all over this world.' And I said, 'You are?' And she said, 'Just watch me and see.'"

In school, too, Oprah was determined not to let her star be dimmed. She started kindergarten in Milwaukee and immediately realized that she was way ahead of the other children, who didn't know how to read or write. Oprah decided to make her teacher aware of this situation by writing her a letter—using her most impressive vocabulary.

"Dear Miss Newe," she wrote, "I do not belong here because I can read and I know a lot of big words like elephant and hippopotamus."

Miss Newe agreed. The next day her teacher had her moved into the first grade. About the incident, the grown-up Oprah said, "What I couldn't articulate then but knew inside was that I could do better. That knowledge has been a constant in my life."

To be fair to Vernita, trying to raise two young children alone was no easy task. Coming home after a long bus ride from the suburbs where she cleaned other people's houses tired her out. Only twenty-four years old herself, a young woman who liked to dress fashionably and go out and have a good time, Vernita probably had many moments when she felt overwhelmed by her responsibilities. After only a couple of years, Vernita came to the conclusion that things weren't working out the way she had hoped. Since sending Oprah back to ailing Grandma Hattie in Mississippi was not really an option, she decided that she would call Oprah's father, Vernon Winfrey, who was living in Nashville, Tennessee, to see if he would be willing to have Oprah come and live with him and his wife, Zelma. Vernon agreed.

Now just eight years old, Oprah was on her way to her third home in a third different state. When Vernon Winfrey drove up to Milwaukee to get her in the summer of 1962, he was a virtual stranger to Oprah, and she didn't know Zelma at all. It would have been understandable if Oprah had been upset or confused. Perhaps she had some of those feelings, but when she arrived in Nashville and saw her new home, a small brick house with white shutters, she remembers that the one thing she felt for sure was delight. Instead of a boardinghouse, she was now going to be living in a real home, just like the kind she saw kids living in on TV. She would have her own bedroom! And for the first time in her life, she was going to have a father. "I wanted a father when I was in Milwaukee. I wanted a family like everybody else."

Eventually the hardworking Vernon Winfrey would own a barbershop and a small grocery story, but in 1962 he was working two jobs—as a janitor at Vanderbilt University and as a seventy-five-cent-an-hour dishwasher in a local hospital. He and Zelma were delighted to have Oprah come and live with them because Zelma was unable to have children. However, their happiness at having a daughter didn't stop either one of them from being strict with Oprah right from the start.

Zelma in particular was tough. "I owe a lot to her," acknowledges Oprah. "It was like a military school there."

Yet instinctively, Oprah realized that everything Vernon and Zelma were doing was for her own good. Zelma, for instance, wanted Oprah to be ready for school when it started in the fall. It wasn't enough that Oprah was a good reader. Zelma made her write book reports for the books she read and drilled her on vocabulary lists. When she found out that Oprah wasn't as strong in math as she was in reading, Zelma practiced the multiplication tables with her over and over until her stepdaughter had them down.

Of course, having to read lots of books wasn't exactly a hardship for Oprah. She was thrilled when Zelma took her to get a library card, something Vernita had refused to do. In the library, Oprah found a series of books about a girl named Katie John, a ten-year-old girl who lived in a big old house in the South, and they became her favorites. Like almost every character in children's books in those days, Katie John was white. All of popular culture in those days was dominated by white faces. The television shows that Oprah had enjoyed watching in Milwaukee, like *Leave It to Beaver*, were about white families living in spacious suburban houses with both parents. From what she saw on television, she thought it would be preferable to be a white child because they never seemed to get hit like she did. They got talked to instead. In her new situation in Nashville, complete with two parents and a bedroom, Oprah must have felt like she was living a life closer to what she had admired on TV. Certainly, she blossomed under all the attention she was getting.

In school, she once again skipped a grade. She was starting the fourth grade at the Wharton School, and her teacher was someone who would become very special to her. She ran home after her first day in school to tell her father that she had the best teacher ever. Years later she remembered, "One of the defining moments of my life came in the fourth grade, the year I was Mrs. Duncan's student. What Mrs. Duncan did for me was to help me to not be afraid of being smart. She encouraged me to read, and she often stayed after school to work with me, helping me choose books and letting me help her grade papers. For many years after that, I had one goal—that I would one day become a fourth-grade teacher who would win the teacher award—because I was going to be the best teacher anyone had ever seen!"

Decades later, when Oprah had her own television show in Chicago, her producers brought Mrs. Duncan as a guest on the show. "I hadn't seen her since grade school, and suddenly, I'm reading the teleprompter, 'Welcome, Mary Duncan.' My eyes filled with tears, and I said, 'Mrs. Duncan had a name! Her name is Mary.' As a child, I hadn't even considered that Mrs. Duncan might have had a life beyond our class. It was in her class that I really came into myself. After all these years, I could say thank you to a woman who had a powerful impact on my early life."

Watching the adult Oprah meeting with Mrs. Duncan for the first time since Oprah's stint in the fourth grade made for very tender viewing. Oprah broke down when Mrs. Duncan took her in her arms, and she remembered through her tears how special the teacher had always made her feel.

"Was I your favorite?" Oprah asked her as the audience laughed, seeing how important the answer still was to the now-famous television host.

In her sweet, soft, Southern accent, Mrs. Duncan replied, "Why of course. But I couldn't let anybody else know."

Another woman who made an indelible impression on Oprah, several years later, was Tish Hooker, the wife of John J. Hooker, who ran for governor of Tennessee. The Hookers came to Oprah's church on a campaign stop, and Mrs. Hooker spotted Oprah sitting in the pews. She picked her out of the crowd and told the wide-eyed girl, "You are as pretty as a speckled pup. You have such beautiful bee-stung lips."

Oprah didn't know what bee-stung lips were. She knew she had big lips, but here was this attractive, well-dressed woman complimenting her. Oprah went home after church and stared in the mirror, searching to find that pretty girl that Tish Hooker had seen, and finally she was able to see her, too. In 2004, Oprah's producers surprised her by bringing Tish Hooker on the show. Mrs. Hooker remembered the girl who gave off such a sparkle that she felt obliged to affirm her. Oprah earnestly told Mrs. Hooker that she had remembered that very special moment all her life, because it had made her see herself differently.

While living in Nashville, Oprah was delighted to be able to resume her public speaking. She was a "champion speaker," as she called herself. African American churches, women's groups, and banquets all might find themselves treated to a recitation from little Miss Winfrey. The grown-up Oprah added, "Anybody who needed anybody to speak about anything, they called on me."

All of this attention went to her head. Even Oprah herself recalled, "I believed I could do almost anything. I felt I was the queen bee." The praise she was getting, however, all came from adults. Just like in Mississippi, kids her own age were less impressed. They thought she was a big show-off. "The kids used to poke fun at me all the time," she admits.

The teasing didn't bother Oprah much. She had an identity, and it sprang from her ability to sway people with her words. Looking back on her gift for public speaking, she says, "I was an orator for a long time. I've been an orator really, basically, all of my life. . . . I did all of James Weldon Johnson's sermons. He has a series of seven sermons, beginning with 'The Creation' and ending with 'Judgment.' I used to do them for churches all over the city of Nashville. . . . You sort of get known for that. Other people were known for singing; I was known for talking."

One poem she liked to recite was an inspirational piece called "Invictus," by William Ernest Henley. It begins, "Out of the night that covers me, / black as the Pit from pole to pole, / I thank whatever gods may be / for my unconquerable soul." At the time, Oprah notes, she didn't really know what all the words meant, but she would say them with drama and flourish, and she added hand motions to make her recitation even more impressive. As in Mississippi, people would hear her and say, "Whew, that child can speak." Oprah says, "Whatever you do a lot of, you get good at doing it," and she considers those speeches the real start of her broadcasting career.

Like Hattie Mae, Vernon and Zelma were devoted churchgoers and spent their Sundays at Nashville's Progressive Missionary Baptist Church, and of course, Oprah attended church with them. The services made a big impact on Oprah. "I would listen to everything the preacher said on Sunday and go back to school on Monday and beg Mrs. Duncan to let me do devotions, just repeat some of the sermon." Needless to say, this didn't add to her popularity with her classmates. But Oprah didn't really care. "I was inspired." When the church was trying to raise money for the poor children of Costa Rica, Oprah started a fund-raising campaign, determined to raise more money than anyone else. She gave up her lunch money and convinced other children to do the same through her powers of persuasion, if not her popularity.

Her fund-raising was an offshoot of her strong feelings for the Golden Rule, which she had learned at church. "Do unto others as you would have them do unto you" were words that had power and meaning for Oprah. "I wrote them on everything," she remembered. "And I carried them around in my book satchel. I even thought I was going to be a missionary. Her classmates would run away, saying, "Here comes the preacher." Despite her affection for the Golden Rule, Oprah was hardly a perfect practitioner of it. Faced with a girl who didn't like her, Oprah went around talking behind her back. When one of her friends pointed out that she was not living up to the spirit of the Golden Rule, Oprah said, "I don't care. I don't like her anyway."

Without a doubt, Oprah had a very successful school year with her father and her stepmother in Nashville. But Vernita wanted her home for the summer, so back to Milwaukee she went.

In Oprah's absence, Vernita had managed to scrape together enough money to move her family to a bigger apartment with three rooms. But she also became pregnant with another child, Oprah's half-brother, Jeffrey. She hoped that Jeffrey's father would marry her, but that was not to be. For reasons of her own, Vernita decided that she wanted Oprah to stay in Milwaukee after the summer visit was over. When Vernon drove up to Milwaukee to get Oprah in time for the start of school, Vernita informed him that he had no legal rights to the girl. Vernon, upset and angry, was forced to return to Nashville without his daughter: "We had brought her out of that atmosphere, out of a house into a home, so I knew it was not good for her, being in that environment again."

Oprah couldn't have been very happy, either. Instead

of the being the center of attention, she was now one of three children. Although she still spent all the hours she could curled up with a book, watching over her sister and brother took up much of her free time. The strict but warm family atmosphere she had known with her father had been replaced by an unsettled existence where her mother was often away working, and adult relatives and friends of Vernita drifted in and out of the apartment.

Life wasn't looking much like a television show now.

Three

"I FIRST LEARNED about sex the year I was nine. I was living in Milwaukee . . . when a nineteen-year-old cousin raped me. As I trembled and cried, he took me for ice cream and convinced me not to tell . . . and for twelve years I didn't."

That is how Oprah Winfrey, many years later, wrote about the most horrible event of her life. And the abuse didn't end with that one incident. "It happened over a period of years between nine and fourteen. It happened at my own house, by different people—this man, that man, a cousin. . . . I remember blaming myself for it, thinking something must be wrong with me."

It wasn't until Oprah was an adult that she understood how completely her life had changed from the moment she was first raped. Worse than just physical pain was the psychological trauma that she went through for decades after; the weight of the secret she had to keep was almost more than she could bear. Oprah's preteen years were shrouded in shame and the fear that she was a bad girl. The most intense feeling she carried with her throughout that time, however, was of being utterly and miserably alone.

After she became a famous television personality, Oprah would use these experiences to help other children who found themselves in the same situation, but during the 1960s, when Oprah was being abused, the subject was not discussed much publicly. She didn't confide in anyone because she didn't think she would be believed—or if she was, people would assume that the abuse was somehow her own fault. So Oprah kept quiet about what was happening to her and began living two distinct lives. The one at home was filled with fear and shame, but at school she did what she always did to prove that she was special. She excelled at her schoolwork.

What she did not do was make many friends. It was as if she didn't want other children to get too close to her and learn her secrets. Still, she hung around with the kids at school enough to hear them talking about where babies came from. Even though Oprah had experienced sex, she did not really know the facts of life, and when she made the connection between what was happening to her and pregnancy, she was horrified. Now every time she got a stomach-ache, she wondered if the pain meant that she was pregnant. The stress must have been unrelenting.

The school that Oprah was attending during her preteen years was located in a rough neighborhood in downtown Milwaukee, and it had a primarily minority attendance. Sometimes fistfights broke out among the students, but Oprah tried to stay away from trouble, spending most of her time by herself, reading when-ever possible. She might have thought that no one noticed her, but one teacher did. Eugene Abrams would see Oprah Winfrey alone in the cafeteria read-ing a book and wonder about her. He learned that she was a good student, someone with the potential to make her dreams into reality, and he thought he had a way to help her. As Mrs. Duncan had, another teacher stepped in at a crucial moment to make a difference in Oprah's life.

Gene Abrams was aware of a new program called

Upward Bound. It had begun only two years earlier, and it was set up by the federal government to help bright children from disadvantaged households get on an educational path that would lead them to college. Along with financial aid and counseling, the program provided scholarships to higher achieving schools. Oprah was offered a scholarship to Nicolet High School in the upper-middle-class Milwaukee suburb of Glendale. She accepted.

Oprah has said that whenever she hears Paul Simon's song "Born at the Right Time," she thinks he must be singing about her. In the backdrop of her young life, huge changes in race relations were going on throughout the United States. In 1954, when Oprah was born, her home state of Mississippi was among the most segregated in the United States; even drinking fountains and bathrooms there were divided by race. So were the schools, which were supposed to be separate but equal, yet this was hardly the case. All too often, the schools for black children were in disrepair, and although most of the teachers did their best, they were sometimes undereducated for their jobs. The classrooms of even the better teachers suffered from a lack of textbooks and the most basic materials.

But things were about to change. That same year, 1954, the Supreme Court ruled on the case of *Brown v. Board of Education*. In that landmark case, the Supreme Court declared unanimously that "separate educational facilities are inherently unequal," thus opening the way to integrated schools. It was slow going. Throughout the late 1950s and 1960s, integrating the public schools, especially in the South, led to bitter clashes between blacks and whites, and between the federal and the state governments. The Civil Rights Act, signed into federal law in 1964, and the Voting Rights Act of 1965 helped pave the way for minorities to be protected from discriminatory treatment. In her later life, other pushes to make American society more inclusive would benefit Oprah, but for now, the way society was evolving gave her the opportunity to go to a better school.

There was an upside and a downside to Oprah's move, however. Yes, she was now at a school that challenged her scholastically, but it was twenty-five miles away from her home. Every morning, she had to travel on three buses to get to Nicolet. Many of her fellow bus riders were maids—like her mother—going into the suburbs to clean white people's homes.

Nineteen sixty-eight, the year Oprah began as a freshman at Nicolet, was a pivotal year in American history. The country was in turmoil after the assassinations of Martin Luther King Jr. and Robert F. Kennedy, and angrily divided over the Vietnam War. The Civil Rights Movement had brought together whites and blacks, many idealistic young people among them, who were determined to fight for change. Yet by the late 1960s, this coalition began fraying.

Oprah must have worried a bit about how she would be received at a school where she was a "bus kid," practically the only student of color in a sea of white. It was less than ten years earlier that nine black teenagers had integrated Little Rock High School in Arkansas, only to spend a year facing verbal and physical abuse. But Oprah was not treated badly. In fact, she was something of an attraction. A number of the kids thought it was cool to have a black friend, and they would invite her over after school or to stay at their houses on the weekend. Mostly out of curiosity,

Oprah Winfrey's freshman-year photo at Nicolet High School in 1968.

Oprah went, and what she saw in other girls' homes made for an unhappy comparison with her own. For the first time in her life, Oprah got to see how people with money lived: the big houses, the nice cars, the maids keeping everything bright and clean. It was probably a bitter thought for Oprah that Vernita could easily be the woman scrubbing and sweeping her new friends' houses.

Sometimes a kid would even trot out the maid to

meet Oprah, figuring that they must know each other because they were both black. In that same vein, a classmate might ask her if she knew popular African American entertainers of the day like Sammy Davis Jr. Oprah didn't know whether to laugh or cry at such naïvety. She did know that her experience in the suburbs was making her jealous.

"The life I saw those children lead was so totally different from what I went home to, from what I saw when I took the bus home with the maids in the evening. I wanted my mother to be like their mothers. I wanted my mother to have cookies ready for me when I came home and to say, 'How was your day?' But she was one of those maids."

As an adult, Oprah was able to understand that life wasn't easy for her mother, either. Hardworking, tired, "her way of showing love to me was . . . putting clothes on my back, and having food on the table." At the time, however, Oprah felt more anger at her situation than she did sympathy for her mother.

There are probably many reasons that Oprah began acting out when she was a teenager. Lots of teens are rebellious, but sexually abused children, especially those who are keeping their secret, often become out of control. This was what was happening to Oprah, who began doing all the wrong things. She now started choosing her sexual partners, older boys whom she stayed out late with. When she became angry that she couldn't afford the nice clothes or extras her classmates took for granted, like going to the movies or eating out, she stole money out of her mother's purse—and if she got caught, she lied about it. "I caused all kinds of problems for myself," Oprah noted ruefully.

One incident was almost funny. Oprah needed glasses, and the most inexpensive frames her mother could find were very unhip butterfly frames. At first, Oprah tried to reason with her mother. "I felt so bad about wearing these glasses that I said to my mother one day, I said, 'Mom, I think [we] need to talk about this because I'm really an ugly child.'" But Vernita simply couldn't afford different glasses, so one day when her mother was out, Oprah went to Plan B. She stomped on the glasses, messed up the apartment, and called the police, yelling, "We've been robbed!"

Oprah had already harbored a secret desire to

become an actress, and she played this role to the hilt. When the police arrived, she lay crumpled on the floor, seemingly unconscious. She didn't quite convince the police, but they took her to the hospital anyway, where the doctor called Vernita, who rushed to Oprah's side.

Vernita was told by a police officer that there seemed to be nothing missing from the apartment and that the only thing broken was a pair of glasses. Oh, and one other thing: Oprah was claiming she had amnesia.

Broken glasses? Amnesia? Vernita marched into her daughter's hospital room, where Oprah looked up at her blankly.

"I hear you have amnesia," Vernita said.

"I can't remember anything," Oprah agreed.

"Well, I'm going to give you three seconds to remember," Vernita told her firmly.

Oprah fluttered her eyes a little. She knew the game was up. "It's coming back to me. . . . You're my mother."

Vernita was mad, but she grudgingly appreciated the lengths Oprah would go to in order to get a rid of the hated glasses. Since the old ones were broken anyway, she wound up buying her daughter a more attractive pair.

The glasses incident had some humor to it, but not much else in Oprah's life was funny. Oprah began fighting with her mother over everything, and when things got really heated, she would run away. In an ironic twist of fate, Oprah Winfrey, who would interview practically every famous person in the world as an adult, had her first brush with celebrity during one of these disappearances. Oprah had arranged to sleep over at a girlfriend's house, but unexpectedly the girl and her family went away for the weekend. At loose ends, Oprah decided she still didn't want to go home. Then she saw a white limo parked on the street of downtown Milwaukee—and who should be sitting inside but the famous singer, the Queen of Soul, Aretha Franklin.

Without missing a beat, Oprah spun a tale of woe for Franklin: her parents had thrown her out of the house, and she desperately needed to get to relatives in Ohio. Apparently, Oprah's acting talent had kicked in once again, because Aretha Franklin was moved and gave the teenager a hundred dollars. That was enough for Oprah to get herself a room in a nearby hotel where she would chill out for the next couple of days. When the money ran out, Oprah was smart enough to call the family pastor to help smooth over the situation so she could go home.

But even the pastor couldn't keep her there. Mother and daughter were at each other constantly. Vernita was fed up with Oprah and realized that their home situation wasn't working out for either of them. She made the drastic decision that she was going to send Oprah to a home for wayward girls, where she might get the discipline and structure that she so obviously needed. Despite all the travail with her mother over the years, fourteen-year-old Oprah was shocked. She distinctly remembers thinking at the time, *I am a smart girl. How did I get here?*

Then, in what turned out to be a very lucky break, the home Oprah was headed to didn't have any beds available, and would not for several weeks. Vernita couldn't wait. She wanted Oprah out of the house, and she wanted her gone as soon as possible. To that end—once again—she called Vernon to come and get his daughter. Looking back, Oprah was able to say that Vernon's willingness to take her back to Nashville saved her life. But she was going back to Nashville with a secret.

Four

WHEN OPRAH ARRIVED in Nashville, Vernon and her stepmother, Zelma, were glad to have her back, but they didn't like the changes they saw in the girl. Oprah was now a teenager who had a sassy mouth and a slippery relationship with the truth. The first change Vernon made in Oprah's attitude was to insist that she call him "Father" or "Dad," not her casual "Pops." Little did he know that there was a much bigger problem looming than how his daughter addressed him. Fourteen-year-old Oprah was pregnant.

It is unclear how long Oprah knew of her condition. The girl who thought every stomachache might be a pregnancy probably lived in denial for a while. Even after she had figured out what was happening to her expanding body, she didn't tell anyone, wearing loose clothing to hide the pregnancy. Vernon and Zelma

UP CLOSE: OPRAH WINFREY

didn't find out that Oprah was seven months pregnant until the day she went into premature labor. The baby boy she delivered lived for just two weeks.

The pregnancy, birth, and death shocked Oprah. So much so that she never talked about it, keeping it an intensely personal secret. Only after she became famous did the story leak out, when her half-sister, Patricia, sold it to a tabloid newspaper. The betrayal was so great and so upsetting, it made the adult Oprah, as she put it, "take to [her] bed." When she was finally able to talk about it, she said, "I hid my pregnancy until the day the child was born. And I named all the people who could possibly have been responsible."

Oprah was not sure who fathered her baby. The last person to abuse her had been an uncle, but she had been with teenage boys as well. She learned later that her mother, too, had carried her "in shame," and was not one hundred percent sure Vernon was Oprah's father. In 2006 Oprah took part in a PBS TV series called *African American Lives*, which traced her family through DNA, although it's not clear that her father was tested. As far as Oprah is concerned, however, Vernon "honored me by taking me in . . . and over the years, people have said, 'Well, I don't know if he really is your dad.' But he is the only father I know. He took responsibility for me when he didn't have to. So my father saved my life at a time when I needed to be saved."

As it turned out, Vernon was the perfect person to help Oprah pick up the pieces of her young life. Even though his only experience with fathering had come the year Oprah had lived with him before, he had firm ideas about how children should be raised, and he could provide the structure so lacking in his daughter's life. Oprah herself later said, "My father's discipline channeled my need for love and affection in a new direction. . . . He knew what he wanted and expected and he would take nothing else." Or as Vernon more colloquially put it, "If I tell you a mosquito can pull a wagon, don't ask me no questions. Just hitch him up!"

Oprah was smart enough to know that, had the baby lived, as an unwed teenage mother her choices in life would have been severely compromised. Her sadness at the death of her child was probably mixed with relief. If a second chance was being offered, she was ready to take it.

The changes started with her look. Friends who had known Oprah in Milwaukee might have had trouble recognizing her in Nashville. The tight clothes and the heavy makeup were gone. Now she dressed demurely, in pleated skirts and long-sleeved blouses. Her hairstyle was a plain flip with a head-band to hold it in place. Perhaps symbolically, to show that she was starting over, she began using her middle name, Gail, as a nickname.

In September 1968, Oprah started the tenth grade at Nashville's East High School. East High was one of the first schools in Nashville to be integrated, and Oprah's graduating class, the class of 1971, was only the second to have blacks and whites in attendance together. The experience was much different than it had been at Nicolet, where Oprah was an oddity. Here, she was part of a group of African American students, who altogether made up about 30 percent of the school. Oprah was one of the popular kids, with friends of both races.

At first, however, she wasn't the star student that she had been the last time she lived in Nashville, bringing home grades that were mostly Cs. Despite her recent trauma, Vernon and Zelma weren't about to cut the girl any slack. Vernon told her, "If you were a child who could only get Cs, then that's what I would expect of you. But you are not. So in this house, Cs are not acceptable."

With that push, Oprah buckled down to her studies once more. Just as they had when she was nine years old, Zelma and Vernon insisted that she read books and write reports on them. Vernon's feeling about the importance of education may have originated from hearing stories about his great-grandfather, Constantine Winfrey, who once had a school for "colored children" moved to his property when it was slated for demolition.

One of Oprah's favorite books was Betty Smith's *A Tree Grows in Brooklyn*, about a girl with a troubled family life growing up in the early part of the twentieth century. "I had a tree in my backyard, too, so I identified with her. I just felt, this is my life, too." However, the book that had the most profound effect on the teenager's life was Maya Angelou's *I Know Why the Caged Bird Sings*. "Well, first of all, it was the first time I had ever encountered another woman who had been sexually abused." She later added, "It was the first book

I ever read that made me feel my life as a colored girl growing up in Mississippi deserved validation."

Vernon and Zelma also were supportive when Oprah once again took up her public speaking, which had brought her such positive attention when she had last lived in Nashville. Vernon understood that she had great potential. "We knew she had a gift and talent to act and to speak. She's never been a backseat person, in school or in church. She always loved the limelight."

And the limelight loved her. Before long, she was once again attracting the positive attention that had brought her such self-esteem before the troubled years she spent in Milwaukee. Vernon was a deacon at Progressive Missionary Baptist Church, and Oprah got involved with the church doings right from the start. To raise money for new robes for the church choir, she organized a series of presentations at local churches, based on the sermons in James Weldon Johnson's *God's Trombones*. Oprah would wow the audiences with her interpretation of the most dramatic sermon, "The Crucifixion."

One of the church deacons, Carl Adams, said of

Oprah, "She could just about hold you spellbound. She would always give something that was fulfilling spiritually."

One particularly exciting event happened when Oprah was sixteen. A pastor from Los Angeles heard her speak in Nashville. He was so impressed with what he heard, he asked her to come out to speak at his church—and offered her a five-hundred-dollar payment. This was a huge event in Oprah's life. Not only did she have the honor of being asked to speak, she was getting to go to glamorous Hollywood, where she had her first taste of what a star's life would be like. As part of her L.A. sightseeing, she was taken to Grauman's (now Mann's) Chinese Theatre, where she saw the famous hand- and footprints of movie stars in concrete. Oprah came back to Nashville and informed her father that someday she was going to be recognized as a star, too. Vernon didn't disagree. He, too, thought that someday she might be famous.

But Oprah wasn't only living in the future. She was having lots of fun in high school, as well. She was an active member of the East Nashville's forensics team, which combined debate and public speaking, and as a senior she ran for vice president of the student body. Her slogan was "Vote for Grand Old Oprah," playing off the name of one of Nashville's biggest attractions, the country music hall, the Grand Ole Opry. Her winning platform promised better food in the school cafeteria and a live band at the senior prom. For her seventeenth birthday, she took over the school gym and invited everyone in her senior class.

Senior year was also when Oprah began dating her first serious boyfriend, a fellow senior, Anthony Otey. When it came to boys, Vernon had told her that once she began to respect herself, boys would respect her, too. When Anthony and Oprah—or Gail—began dating, they decided to be cautious in their physical relationship, restricting themselves to kissing. Years later, when Anthony learned about Oprah's sexual abuse and promiscuity, and the birth of her baby, he was shocked. Their relationship was romantic, not sexual.

Anthony met Oprah at the local community center, but he was also one of the African American students integrating East Nashville High. As an adult, he remembered the first moment he saw his future girlfriend. "She had these pigtails and this guy and I were

Oprah Winfrey during her senior year at Nashville's East High School in 1971.

working the door at the Fred Douglass Community Center. She watched all these kids dancing, and the guys kept saying, 'Who's that girl?'"

Once they started dating, Anthony was so smitten with Oprah that he almost immediately wrote her a long note asking her to be his girlfriend. Oprah put him off at first, airily telling him, "Regarding your question—if the offer still stands—I refuse to answer right now simply because the atmosphere is so blah."

This was one of hundreds of notes that Anthony and Oprah wrote to each other during their senior year. They'd write them at night and then pass them to each other the next morning. Oprah might write about how much she loved him, adding that even though her father didn't understand their love, she was sure God did. Anthony was equally romantic. One of his notes said, "I got a feeling this day is going to be great. And do you know why? Go on, guess. . . . This day is going to be beautiful and great because I'm in love with you. Has anybody ever told you that a day without you is like a day without sunshine? Smile!" Since Anthony was artistic, he'd add little drawings to his notes.

Oprah and Anthony had fun doing simple things:

going to Shelby Park and hanging out with their friends, feeding the ducks, and tossing Frisbees. More formal dates were spent eating out at Pizza Hut and Burger King and going to the movies. They had a song that was "theirs," Simon and Garfunkel's "Bridge over Troubled Water," and their own secret love codes. Instead of saying, "I love you," in public, they'd tell each other, "The green grass is growing all around."

It hadn't been easy to convince Vernon Winfrey that Anthony and Oprah should be allowed to go steady, and he set rules for the relationship that the couple had to follow to the letter. Anthony had to pick Oprah up at the house, and any date had to be over by eleven P.M. At 11:01, Vernon would head out to look for them. If they stayed home, a parent always had to be in attendance. Despite the restrictions on their relationship, Anthony and Oprah planned a future together. They talked about getting married and having a family someday. But Anthony later said that he knew they were just dreaming. He could feel that Oprah was going places, and that he probably wasn't going with her. "One thing I remember most about Gail is that she knew what she wanted very early in life. She said that she wanted to be a movie star. She wanted to be an actress. . . . She knew what she wanted to do, worked hard at it, and when her ship came in, she jumped aboard."

It's easy to see why Anthony felt this way. It was as if every time Oprah turned around, she met with some new accolade or success. Around the same time as her trip to Los Angeles, Oprah was chosen to represent her high school at a White House Conference on Youth in Estes Park, Colorado. The conference brought together outstanding teenagers and business leaders to discuss issues of interest to America's youth. A little later, she won a speech contest sponsored by the local African American Elks Club. The prize was a four-year college scholarship. Then, in her senior year, something happened that set her firmly on the road to her ultimate destiny.

It all began with a March of Dimes Walk-a-Thon. Oprah needed a local business to sponsor her, so she went to a radio station, WVOL, to see if she could muster up any support. A disc jockey, John Heidelberg, agreed to sponsor her, but instead of just telling her to come back after the Walk-a-Thon to collect her money, he asked her if she would like to hear her voice on tape. There was something about her bubbly, confident personality and the impressive way she spoke that made him think that this teenager just might have a voice for radio.

Thirty years later, John Heidelberg, now the owner of the station, appeared on the *Oprah* show. They laughed about how he had put her into the recording booth, ripped some news copy off the wire, and told her to read. Oprah said she wasn't fazed a bit. After all her experience, she knew she could read well. Her audition was so impressive, Heidelberg called in other people from the station to hear her, and as Oprah remembers it, she was offered a job that very day.

Of course, she knew better than to just accept. She told the station manager to call her father, and Vernon wasn't easy to convince. For one thing, he had added a small grocery store adjacent to the barbershop he owned, and Oprah worked there. He wasn't thrilled about having to replace his daughter with an employee he'd have to pay more. After he heard the station manager's offer, however, there was no way he could stand in his daughter's way. WVOL was offering one hundred dollars a week for a part-time job reading the news after school. Oprah was excited about getting a job in broadcasting—and thrilled she didn't have to work at the grocery store anymore.

Oprah's senior year was coming to a close. She was voted Most Popular Girl in the senior class. Anthony was voted Most Popular Boy. They went to the senior prom together, but afterward Oprah told him, "We gotta talk." Anthony knew what that meant. Oprah was breaking up with him. Her life was picking up speed, and she was leaving him behind.

In three short years, Oprah Winfrey had seemingly turned into a different girl. Or maybe she'd just gone back to being the smart, self-directed young woman she had always been. In either case, Oprah's career in broadcasting had begun, the road was forward as far as the eye could see, and there was never going to be any looking back.

Five

OPRAH WANTED TO use the college scholarship she had won from the Elks Club to go away to college, but her father insisted that she enroll at Nashville's all-black Tennessee State University. Despite Oprah's extraordinarily successful high-school career, Mr. Winfrey was not ready to let his daughter out of his sight. Oprah wasn't very happy about staying home for college, especially since the school had no radio or TV departments; she would have to major in speech and drama instead. Nevertheless, she acceded to her father's wishes and agreed to continue living at home; extra spending money would come from her job at WVOL.

The radio station had offered her another opportunity after she had been working there for about six months. WVOL wanted to sponsor a contestant in the Miss Fire Prevention beauty pageant, and they decided Oprah would be a terrific entrant. Oprah was surprised. She was used to getting attention for her public speaking, but she didn't consider herself beauty-contest material. Besides, only white girls had ever won the contest. Still, she figured she had nothing to lose, so she agreed to enter.

With that attitude, she decided just to have fun at the pageant. "Well, all you had to do was walk, parade around . . . answer some questions about your life. You know, it was one of those little, teeny tiny beauty pageants. Well, nobody expected me to win . . . so I was very relaxed about it. I thought, *I've got a new gown, so this is great.*"

The last segment of the contest consisted of the judges asking each girl the same question: "What would you do with a million dollars?"

For some reason, several of the contestants that year had red hair. The first girl, with long red hair, earnestly told the judges that she would buy her father a new truck.

"I'd buy my mother a Frigidaire refrigerator," the second redhead answered.

Then Oprah stepped up to the microphone. "If I had a million dollars," she began, flashing the judges a big smile, "I would be a spendin' fool. I'm not quite sure what I would spend it on, but I would spend, spend, spend. Spendin' fool."

Oprah Winfrey, winner of the Miss Fire Prevention beauty pageant.

The judges roared with laughter. Oprah was a breath of fresh air, and she won the contest.

Oprah's ongoing job reading the news at WVOL was one of the best parts of her early college years. College itself was a disappointment. "I hated, hated, hated college," she has said. The thing that bothered her most was the militant thinking on black issues that suffused the campus. In the 1950s and 1960s, the focus of the Civil Rights Movement had been integration through nonviolent means. Now segments of the movement were getting angrier and more radical in their philosophy and tactics. None of this appealed to Oprah, and she resented being marginalized by other students on campus for her more inclusive stand.

Oprah was well aware of the importance of her African American heritage. She especially admired Harriet Tubman, a runaway slave who, at great personal sacrifice, led hundreds of other slaves to freedom on the Underground Railroad, and Sojourner Truth, an abolitionist and fighter for women's rights. When she looked in the mirror, she saw a black woman's face staring out at her. Yet perhaps because of her experiences in integrated schools, she did not feel particularly alienated from whites and didn't agree with the perspective that whites were the enemy. "It was in to be angry. Whenever there was any conversation on race, I was on the other side, maybe because I never felt the kind of repression other black people are exposed to."

As usual, despite any unhappiness in her personal life, her educational and professional life surged forward. In 1973, when Oprah was a sophomore at Tennessee State, only nineteen years old, she got a call from Chris Clark, the station manager at WTVF, the CBS affiliate in Nashville. He had heard her on the radio, liked the way she sounded, and thought she might transfer her talents to television. A surprised Oprah turned him down. She didn't think that she could handle a high-pressure TV job and continue her studies at the same time. Besides, she had decided her real dream was to be an actress.

The station manager didn't give up, calling her twice more, insisting that she at least audition for the job. A confused—and flattered—Oprah went to one of her favorite professors, Dr. William Cox, for advice, and as she remembered later, he laughed and called her stupid for turning down the audition. "Don't you know that's why people go to college? So that CBS can call them?"

Oprah had to laugh, too. Suddenly her choice seemed obvious. At the very least, she might as well try out for the job. Although she was an experienced newsreader on the radio, television was something quite different. Oprah didn't really know how she should present herself, so she decided that she would use broadcaster Barbara Walters, the first woman coanchor at the *Today* show, as her role model.

Although there had always been a few women reporters in television, it was mostly a man's profession—a white man's profession. During the 1970s, blacks and women were just starting to make their presence felt in any numbers on TV, due in part to the civil-rights laws and affirmative-action programs that encouraged minority hires throughout the United States. Oprah knew that if she were hired, it would be because by hiring a woman who was black, the station would be saving itself money by getting a "two-fer"—two minorities for the price of one—but that didn't dampen her enthusiasm once she decided to go for the job.

Barbara Walters, Barbara Walters, nineteen-year-old Oprah reminded herself at the audition. She tried to sit the way she thought she remembered Walters sitting, crossing her legs demurely at the ankles, and alternated between looking down at her script and looking into the camera. "You try to have as much eye contact as you can—at least it seemed that way from what I had seen Barbara do."

The station manager, Chris Clark, seemed to think Oprah would have gotten the job even if she hadn't tried to channel Barbara Walters. Right from the start, her personality came through the screen. "It was unbelievable. You looked at Oprah for the first time, and you said, 'This is right. This will work.' It was just one of those things you don't experience very often."

The job Clark offered Oprah was substantial. She was to be the weekend anchor at WTVF, while continuing her studies during the week, and her salary was $15,000 a year—as much as Vernon was making at the barbershop/grocery store. Despite his enthusiasm, Clark knew he was taking a bit of chance with Oprah. Nashville was still a city of the South, and there had never been an African American on the air there. "It was a very racially tense time in Nashville . . . but there was not a complaint. People just accepted her."

Eventually Oprah moved from the weekend spot to coanchoring the nightly news. She had a down-home style that appealed to almost everyone, although there were certainly some white people in Nashville who did not appreciate the inroads blacks were making on American society in general and Nashville in particular. In one telling incident, Oprah was covering a story, and when introduced to a white shopkeeper, she reached out to shake his hand. "We don't shake hands with niggers down here," he said, turning away. Oprah had the perfect response to his use of the offensive epithet. "I bet the niggers are glad!"

Ironically, Oprah's career in television was also further alienating her from her college classmates. Now that she was well known (and well paid), they called her a token—a member of a minority group who is hired so that an organization can claim to be inclusive. The disdain of the other students probably bothered Oprah at least a little, but she had the last laugh. She may have been a token but, she noted, she was a "happy, paid token." At the same time, some of her classmates hit her up for money, and Oprah was generous, loaning cash or picking up the check in restaurants. Later she acknowledged that she probably felt obligated to share the wealth because she had a disease to please, a desire to make other people happy because of her own low self-esteem. Despite her successes, Oprah had not begun to deal with the wounds of her past caused by abuse and an unstable relationship with her mother. She learned later that "until you do, you are literally dragging the weight of your past into your present, and that makes it hard to move forward."

Oprah may not have had that level of self-awareness in 1976, but she was ready to make a move, if not emotionally, then literally. TV executives in Baltimore, Maryland, had seen her television work and extended an offer to come join the ABC affiliate, WJZ.

She was not quite finished with college—she still had her senior project to complete—but Oprah decided that was a loose end to be tied up later. Baltimore was the tenth largest television market in the country, and the job of coanchoring the evening news there was too good to pass up. Besides, she had personal reasons for wanting to leave Nashville. Even though Oprah was over twenty-one, she was still living in her father's house, and chafing under his rules. She didn't really feel free to come and go as she wished. Plus, Oprah wasn't happy in the romance department. She was in the midst of an on-again, off-again relationship with a young man nicknamed Bubba; Oprah was so smitten with him she asked the radio station to give him her job as newsreader when she left for the TV station. As a favor to Oprah, they did, but Bubba had neither the talent nor the drive to succeed. Nor would he commit to Oprah. Professionally and personally, she was in a rut. By the time the job in Baltimore came up in 1976, Oprah's instinct—which she would learn to rely upon more and more as years went by—told her to take it.

Baltimore was a huge change from Nashville for Oprah in every way. As much as she wanted to be liberated from her father's control, she was lonely in a big city that was in no way as warm or welcoming as Nashville. In fact, she found the city so unattractive that the first time she saw the downtown, she cried. Moreover, the pressure to make good was tremendous. WJZ had launched a big promotional campaign around their new star's arrival. Billboards went up around the city and posters were plastered on buses, asking one question in big letters: "What's an Oprah?"

Baltimore learned the answer when Oprah Winfrey began coanchoring the newly expanded six o'clock news with a longtime Baltimore favorite, Jerry Turner. Turner, a man a number of years older than Oprah, didn't want a coanchor, especially a young woman with much less experience. A traditional newsreader, he didn't inject himself into his newcasts other than to project an air of authority. But Oprah, who thought that she had been hired to bring the folksy demeanor to her broadcasts that had been her trademark in Nashville, had a completely different style. There, she had used the teleprompter sparingly, glancing over at it to get the gist of the story, and then reporting it in her own words. Neither Jerry Turner nor the station executives wanted Oprah to go off script, which made her feel awkward and constrained as she read the news. One night, after mispronouncing the word "Canada" (several times!), she joked about it, prompting the station manager to tell her not to call attention to her mistakes.

If Jerry Turner and the station management weren't

particularly welcoming to Oprah, neither was the Baltimore audience; her presence wasn't doing much to boost the show's ratings. The answer to the question "What's an Oprah?" seemed to be "a broadcaster no one is very impressed with." Oprah was shocked at this unexpected turn of events. "I was devastated. Up until that point, I had sort of cruised." Things went from bad to worse when the station manager who had hired Oprah moved on to another job. Without a staunch defender, it seemed to be open season on the young newscaster.

Since the station had a contract with Oprah, they had to figure out what to do with her. After yanking her off the nightly news, they tried her out as a street reporter. That meant that the station's assignment editor would send her out each day to cover the stories the newsroom thought were important. As it turned out, management liked her even less as a reporter than they did as an anchor.

Their biggest gripe was that she was too emotional and had too much empathy for the people she was supposed to interview, many of whom had just gone through traumatic events, including crimes and other disasters. Things came to a head when Oprah was sent to cover a horrendous house fire that took the lives of several young children. When Oprah arrived at the scene, the distraught mother was there, but Oprah refused to interview her. She couldn't bear to intrude on the woman's grief. Back at the station, the news producer was furious; as far as he was concerned, the mother's reaction to the tragedy *was* the story. He ordered Oprah to do the interview and she complied, but she apologized to the woman and to her audience on the air.

As if having her work denigrated wasn't bad enough, management next started in on her looks. Oprah had been considered pretty enough in college to win the Miss Black Tennessee contest, which secured her a place in the national contest. She was never thin, but she was not overweight, either. However, she did have a tendency to turn to food for comfort when she was in stressful situations, and now that she was unhappy at work, the numbers on the scale were going up. Already Oprah was naturally feeling self-conscious about her weight gain when her overall appearance was given a scathing review by the assistant news director: "Your hair's too long. It's too thick. Your eyes are too far apart. Your nose is too wide. And you need to do something about it."

Actually, the station had an idea about one way to tackle the problem of Oprah's looks. They sent her to New York to what she later called a "chi-chi, pooh-pooh salon." Oprah asked the hairdresser if he knew how to work with African American hair, and he assured her he did. He didn't. "In a week I was bald," Oprah remembered. "I had a French perm and it all fell out. Every little strand. I was left with three little squiggles in the front."

Obviously, the first thing Oprah tried to do was to find a wig, but her head was large, and none of the standard wig sizes fit her. Eventually one was found that was suitable, if not especially flattering. Oprah tried to find the bigger lesson in this disaster. "I went through a real period of self discovery." She learned that "you have to find other reasons for appreciating yourself. It's certainly not your looks."

WJZ also sent Oprah to a speech coach, which she found particularly insulting since she'd been making her way on speeches and recitations since she'd been a child. But Oprah was scared. She knew she was on the verge of being fired, especially after the station took her off the street-reporter assignment and put her on at five thirty A.M. "They tried to convince me at the time that, 'You are so good that you need your own time period, so we are going to give you five minutes at five thirty in the morning.'" Oprah wasn't fooled. She knew that unless the station found something to do with her, she'd soon be leaving WJZ.

But a break was about to come her way. Oprah Winfrey doesn't believe much in luck. She thinks "luck is preparation meeting opportunity." If that's true, she was more than ready for it when a change in management worked to her advantage.

In 1977, yet another station manager came to WJZ. One of the things Bill Carter wanted to do was try a morning talk show, a popular format that helped viewers start their day with a mix of news, weather, traffic, and guest interviews. He quickly realized that he had two potential hosts already working at his station. Richard Sher, one of the other news anchors, had a lively personality, and Carter thought he could pair Sher with the warm, friendly Oprah on a show called *People Are Talking*. Unfortunately, the only time period the station had available to put on *People Are Talking* was opposite *The Phil Donahue Show*, the most popular talk show in the country.

The Donahue show was syndicated, which means that although it originated in Chicago, it was shown all over the country. Phil Donahue, a smart man with glasses and a trademark thatch of white hair, had made a big impression on the viewing audience. Although he interviewed celebrities and did shows about lighthearted topics, he also opened up the discussion to many issues that hadn't been touched on daytime talk shows, such as reproductive rights. He was noted for taking his microphone into the audience—a technique that Oprah would later use to great advantage.

Oprah knew that going up against Donahue would make for a tough ratings battle, but she was too excited to focus on that. On a talk show, she would be free to be herself—no worries about whether she could laugh if she mispronounced a word or cry if she was touched by someone's story. Her luck was about to change, or in Oprah-speak, preparation was ready to crash into opportunity.

Oprah remembers that first show on August 14, 1978, very well. The guests were an ice-cream manufacturer and an actor from the soap opera *All My Children*. When the show was over, Oprah felt like she had been reborn. "I said to myself, this is what I should be doing. It's like breathing."

People Are Talking became an almost immediate success. Richard Sher and Oprah were a study in contrast. Sher was a skinny white man; she was a plump African American woman—although amusingly, they had similar hairstyles, a cap of tight curls, his white, hers black. Sher, a Baltimore native, related well to the hometown audience with his knowledge of the city. Oprah crossed racial lines doing her thing, reaching right into the camera and grabbing viewers with her personable style. They clicked, and the show clicked with the viewers. Amazingly, they were soon beating *The Phil Donahue Show* locally in the ratings.

The show's producer, Sherry Burns, wasn't surprised. She thought Oprah "was a universal woman. She gets right past the black thing. She's a totally approachable, real, warm person." Burns felt the key to the show's success was letting Oprah be herself and utilize her ability to ask the questions people wanted to have answered. In Baltimore, people were talking about Oprah.

Along with her professional success, Oprah was pleased to be making several close friends. One was Maria Shriver, a news anchor at WJZ and a niece of President John Kennedy. Maria would go on to a successful television career, and later she would wed action star Arnold Schwarzenegger, a future governor of California. Another was Gayle King, a young woman who would come to be known to the world as Oprah's best friend. Gayle, a lowly production assistant at WJZ, did not have much contact with Oprah, who had the much higher position as on-screen talent. As Oprah remembered it, they didn't become friends right away. "Then, one night after a big snowstorm, Gayle couldn't get home, so I invited her to stay at my place. Her biggest concern? Underwear." She was determined to drive forty miles through a snowstorm so she'd have clean clothes for the next day. Oprah convinced Gayle to stay over, and they stayed up until the wee hours talking. "And with the exception of a few times during vacations spent out of the country, Gayle and I talked every day since."

It was Gayle who tried to help Oprah with a big problem she was having with her boyfriend. Oprah was involved with man who was married, and the situation grew progressively more painful. At one point, Oprah even considered suicide, writing Gayle a long good-bye note. As she started in on a paragraph about how to take care of her plants, Oprah realized she was being overly dramatic—she had no intention of killing herself. But even if she could see how ludicrous her personal life had become, it was still painful, and she seemed powerless to change it. Gayle was always there to point out when a man was just chipping away at her spirit. "One day I hope he chips deep enough for you to see who you really are—someone who deserves to be happy."

After six years in Baltimore, an amazing opportunity came Oprah's way. One of the producers of *People Are Talking* moved to Chicago for a job on the morning talk show there. When the host of that show left unexpectedly, the producer showed a tape of Oprah to the station manager, Dennis Swanson, who asked Oprah to come for an audition. He saw what so many others had seen: a unique personality that easily captivated audiences with her charisma.

Oprah wondered if she should leave the sure thing that she had going in Baltimore to take a chance in the third largest television market in the country—where once again, she would be an unknown. One of the most worrisome things about taking the job of hosting *A.M. Chicago*—no cohost this time—was that she would again be going head-to-head with Phil Donahue, but this time on his home turf. Gayle, supportive as ever, told her, "You should go to Chicago! You can beat Donahue—I know you can."

"Beat Donahue?" Oprah exclaimed. "That's impossible. That's not even a goal."

Six

OPRAH WINFREY STARTED as the host of *A.M. Chicago* on January 2, 1984. A curly-haired woman in a big fur coat, she introduced herself outside the WLS-TV studios with the University of Illinois marching band blaring out a welcome behind her. Chicago had little time to ask itself, "What's an Oprah?" She took the city by storm, and within a month, almost everyone in the city knew who she was.

Oprah had auditioned for the job in the fall of 1983. Station manager Dennis Swanson had her sit in front of a camera and chat about herself and her interests. After she was finished, Oprah met with Swanson in his office. Even though he was delighted with her audition, he felt that he couldn't totally show his enthusiasm. After all, he was going to have to negotiate a salary with her as soon as he offered her the job.

"How do you think it went?" Oprah asked.

"I think it went pretty well," he replied. But he was thinking that Oprah's was the greatest audition tape he had ever seen.

After he offered her the job—at a salary of about $200,000 a year—Oprah came back with a few concerns of her own. She was worried because she had been told a good deal of racism existed in Chicago. And she also wanted to make sure that Swanson had no intention of putting her through a demeaning makeover like the one she'd had to endure in Baltimore.

"You know, I'm black," she said to him.

"I'm looking at you," Swanson replied.

"And you know I have these kind of weight issues. I have been trying to lose weight," she assured him.

"And so have I. Nobody around here is going to complain about that."

Swanson told her he had only one concern.

"What's that?" Oprah asked worriedly.

Swanson walked over to her and pretended to measure her head with his hands. "Your head fits very nicely on your shoulders. I just want to make sure that when this great success befalls you, it won't get too big."

Oprah was taken aback. "Do you really think I could be that successful?"

"I do."

Dennis Swanson proved to be a prophet. Oprah's success was breathtaking in both its breadth and its speed.

For people living in Chicago at the time, it seemed as if one day Oprah wasn't there and the next she was everywhere. What she had thought was an impossible goal—beating *The Phil Donahue Show* in its hometown and in the same time slot—happened within a couple of weeks. Donahue, who had recently married the actress Marlo Thomas, decided within a year after Oprah came to town to move his show to New York, where his wife lived. His stated reason was to be closer to Marlo, and that was no doubt true, but some people wondered if being in the same town as the Oprah show was just too close for comfort.

Whatever reservations Oprah had about coming to Chicago quickly disappeared. She said, "Just walking down the street, it was like roots, like the motherland. I knew I belonged here."

Pretty soon, she couldn't walk down the street without people coming up to her, talking, sharing their stories. It became a problem. Oprah recalls being in the bathroom at O'Hare Airport when a woman stuck a piece of paper under the stall for her to autograph.

At first, the attention was only local. A.M. *Chicago* was not syndicated—so it wasn't seen around the country. Within a year of Oprah's arrival in Chicago, however, both the ABC network and a company called King World wanted to syndicate her show. Oprah asked advice from Roger Ebert, the well-known, well-respected movie critic of the *Chicago Sun-Times*, who already had a TV show in syndication.

Ebert had first met Oprah when he and his TV-show partner, Gene Siskel, were guests on *People Are Talking*. The other guests included a vegetarian chef and four dwarfs dressed as chipmunks scheduled to sing "The Chipmunk Christmas Song" while dancing with hula hoops. Siskel had implored Ebert not to laugh at the chipmunks or he'd start laughing, too, and perhaps not be able to stop.

A few months after Oprah moved to Chicago, she and Roger Ebert, who also lived in the city, went out to dinner. She told him about her syndication predicament. He did some simple arithmetic on a napkin using his own syndication deal for his show *At the Movies* as an example. Since she would be on five times a week instead of one, as he was, and since she didn't have a partner, as Ebert did, she would make a lot more money in a syndication deal with King World than if she just let ABC buy her show and syndicate it with most of the profits going back to the network. Thanks to Roger Ebert's advice, Oprah eventually decided to sign with King World. When the deal went through in 1986, it helped her become one of the richest women in the world after her show was syndicated, first around the nation and eventually across the globe.

The shows that Oprah did for her first several years in Chicago followed a pattern similar to those she had been doing in Baltimore. There might be a cooking segment or a discussion with psychics. Sometimes a celebrity came to promote a book or a movie. Oprah was thrilled to interview some of her heroes, like singer Stevie Wonder, and her television role model Barbara Walters. But interspersed with these popular-culture pieces, Oprah would also discuss serious topics that meant something to her personally, such as child abuse. Sometimes she would use her show to discuss her own history and problems.

Another talk-show host, Maury Povich, said, "Talk-show hosts didn't talk about themselves. Oprah opened up a lot of new windows because viewers could empathize with her."

When her guests discussed personal traumas and other difficult subjects, Oprah would often lean over

Oprah Winfrey in her studio office at A.M. Chicago on December 18, 1985.

and pat a guest's hand or give him or her a hug. She said, "My ability to get people to open up is [because] there is a common bond in the human spirit. We want the same things. And I know that."

One of the things that she knew she had in common with many people—mostly women, but plenty of men, too—was a battle with weight. Oprah used to think that she handled stress very well, but that was turning out not to be true. The proof was in the pudding—and the bread, and the cake, and the ice cream. Even though Oprah had told Dennis Swanson she was working on her weight problem, the fact of the matter was that in her first six months or so in Chicago, Oprah had gained twenty pounds.

She had started having problems maintaining her weight while she was still in Baltimore. She went to her first diet doctor there, and years later she still had the canceled check that she wrote to pay him. Even though she was a size eight at the time, she thought she was fat. The doctor put her on a 1,200-calorie diet, and she lost ten pounds in two weeks. Two months later, she had regained twelve. "Thus," she later said, "began . . . the struggle with my body. With myself." Her weight issues were gaining even more prominence in Chicago, just as she was being seen by more and more people. In public, she tried to joke about it, but she was embarrassed by her growing size.

In January 1985, A.M. *Chicago* was lengthened to a hour and renamed *The Oprah Winfrey Show*. After a story about her in *Time* magazine (in which she was called "streetwise, brassy and soulful"), Oprah, who had just turned thirty-one a few days before, was invited to be a guest on *The Tonight Show*, which was hosted that night by comedian Joan Rivers. Rivers was known for her sharp tongue and penchant for making fun of people. Oprah was afraid that Rivers would start in on her weight. Rivers wasn't mean, but she did challenge Oprah to a dieting contest. Since she was skinny (but always talked about how fat she felt she was), Joan Rivers said she would lose five pounds by the spring. Oprah said she would try for twenty. Ironically, something was about to happen that would scuttle all her dieting plans.

Back in Baltimore, Oprah had read a book that had a huge impact on her. It was *The Color Purple* by Alice Walker. The book, which won a Pulitzer Prize in 1983, was about a black woman, Celie, living in the South in the early mid-twentieth century. Abused by her father and her husband, Celie struggles to find her own power in life. Oprah, who identified strongly with the women in the story, loved the book so much that she passed copies of it out to her friends.

When Oprah heard that *The Color Purple* was being made into a movie, directed by Steven Spielberg, she harbored a secret hope that she could somehow be a part of it, although on the face of it the idea seemed an impossibility. Oprah was getting to be well known as a talk-show host, but she certainly wasn't considered an actress.

Then something quite amazing happened. Musician and record producer Quincy Jones, who was co-producing the movie, was in Chicago on business. While in his hotel room one morning, he turned on the TV and happened to flip to *The Oprah Winfrey Show*. Almost immediately, he saw in Oprah the same qualities found in one of the book's main characters—the strong, determined Sofia. Jones called his casting people and told them he wanted to see what Oprah could do on camera.

Within weeks, Oprah was in Los Angeles auditioning for the role. She thought it was a good sign that she read with actor William Pugh, who was playing

Sofia's husband, Harpo, in the movie. "Harpo" is "Oprah" spelled backward.

Although other, more experienced actresses were also trying out for the role of Sofia, director Steven Spielberg would later tell people that Oprah's audition blew him away. Still, it took him some time to get back to her, and Oprah was sure, when she hadn't heard for a while, that she had lost the role.

Shaken by her disappointment, Oprah felt she had to make some changes in her life. She decided to go on a retreat to a spa—or as Oprah bluntly put it, "a fat farm"—to lose some weight and lick her wounds over the loss of the part. She remembers very clearly walking, walking, walking around the facility's track, trying to get ahold of her emotions. Finally she decided all she could do was surrender her feelings to God. "I prayed, 'Lord, I've done my best and now help me accept the result.'" As she walked, she sang the hymn "I Surrender," tears flowing from her eyes. As she was walking, praying, and singing, one of the spa's staff came up to her and told her that she had a telephone call.

It was Steven Spielberg. He wanted to let her know personally that she had gotten the role. Oprah later said it was "the single happiest day of my life." But her willingness to surrender the problem to God, and accept that being in the movie was not meant to be, also had a profound effect on her and how she would come to view future difficulties in her life.

In that phone conversation, Spielberg told Oprah one other thing. If she wanted the role, she was to stop dieting immediately. The Sofia he wanted to see on the screen was a woman as big in body as she was in spirit.

Seven

OPRAH WINFREY WAS in the habit of keeping journals, and she had one with her the whole time she was shooting *The Color Purple* in South Carolina. In a June 1985 entry, she wrote: "This morning I sat in the tree and I watched everyone else work. I had no scenes today, but I can't wait to be here every day. Just being here—seeing everybody, seeing Alice [Walker, the author], Quincy [Jones]—every day. Just being around Quincy makes me feel joy. This is what it feels like to love, I believe. Everything about *The Color Purple* feels like love to me."

It may have felt like love to Oprah, but her bosses in Chicago weren't as enamored, and getting time off to do the movie wasn't easy. Her role in the film as Sofia, a betrayed and battered woman, would take almost two months to shoot, and naturally, WLS-TV was loath to let their new star off the air for that length of time. But Dennis Swanson could also see that Oprah was determined to make the movie. He feared that if he didn't let her go, she might quit altogether.

As it turns out, his fears were justified. Oprah had made up her mind that she was going to be in *The Color Purple*, even if it meant leaving her show. However, it was in the best interest of both parties to come to an agreement, so an arrangement was finally worked out that had reruns and guest hosts filling the daily time slot. But Oprah and her lawyer and manager, Jeff Jacobs, could see that the syndication deal she was still considering at that time was a necessity so that she could have more control over her career.

When *The Color Purple* debuted, it was met with mostly good reviews. It was the first serious film by director Steven Spielberg, who was best known for his action films like *Jaws* and *Raiders of the Lost Ark*; film critics felt he had made a faithful, even soulful movie version of the book. However, some people objected to the negative portrayal of African American men that was threaded throughout the movie, even though the interpretation was true to the book. In both, Harpo, Sofia's husband, and Mister, the husband of the main character, Celie, are depicted as abusive men, but Oprah's feeling was that this was not a movie about black men—it was about what black women endured. "I was surprised to see the way people reacted to *The Color Purple*," she said. "I believe people see what they want to see in a work of

Oprah Winfrey played the role of Sofia in the film adaptation of her favorite book, The Color Purple.

art." She also noted "that what the book did for me and what the movie is doing for other women who are sexually abused, is to point out that you're not the only one."

When the Oscar nominations were announced in early 1986, *The Color Purple* was nominated for eleven awards. One of those nominations went to Oprah Winfrey for Best Supporting Actress. Whatever problems reviewers had with the movie, her performance was universally praised.

The night of the Academy Awards in March of 1986 was a microcosm of the highs and lows in Oprah's life at the time. What could be more exciting than being nominated for one of the highest honors in the acting profession? And for a debut performance! Yet walking down the red carpet—fans screaming, photographers snapping away—was a personal nightmare for Oprah.

All the stress of acting for the first time, hosting her show, and making important business decisions had pushed Oprah to eat and eat some more. Even though she was dressed in a gorgeous bead-trimmed gold-and-ivory dress accented by thousands of dollars' worth of sparkling jewelry, Oprah was focused on one thing—how fat she had become. In her hotel room, she had trouble wriggling into the expensive dress, and now as she waved to the cameras, she was uncomfortable, hardly able to breathe. Later, after she lost the Oscar that night to Anjelica Huston, the disappointed Oprah told a women's magazine, "Perhaps God was saying to me, 'Oprah, you are not winning because your dress is too tight for you to make it up all those steps to receive the statuette.'" This wouldn't be the last time an important event was marred for Oprah because of her weight.

One bright spot in the evening was the tall, handsome man escorting Oprah to the Academy Awards ceremony. His name was Stedman Graham, and his relationship with Oprah Winfrey would continue for decades. Stedman met Oprah soon after she arrived in Chicago, but it took them a while to get to a first date.

Stedman Graham, a former basketball player in the European league, and the father of a young daughter, Wendy, was the founder and executive director of a nonprofit organization, Athletes Against Drugs. He later went on to become an author of success-strategy books and a public speaker. He and Oprah first ran into each other at a charity event in Chicago, and they became friends. After a year or so of traveling in the same circles, Graham asked Oprah out on a date. She said no twice, but when he told her he wouldn't ask her out again, she decided to go out with him. Her friends were worried. They thought that he might be asking her out only because of her fame or her money. But the relationship took hold, and Graham was to remain at Oprah's side through bad times and good.

Reporters, interviewers, and people on the street constantly asked the couple when they were going to be married. Several years after they first started dating, they did become engaged, but a wedding never happened. As Graham explained to television host Larry King in 2003, "She travels and I travel . . . she has her life and I have my life, and it is a big life. So trying to fit marriage into that has been somewhat difficult. And you know, we love each other and care for each other, and that's what's important."

After several bad romantic relationships, Oprah was

glad finally to be in a relationship with a man who would give her love and support. And she was pleased that Graham shared her core beliefs: that success stemmed from confidence in self and perseverance, that faith was important, and that it was important to give back to their community. One of the first things Oprah had done when she arrived in Chicago was involve herself and her staff in a Big Sisters program. Oprah felt it was important to take girls out of the housing projects for visits to museums and libraries, and in the process point them toward the possibility of another way of life. She was particularly insistent on letting the "little sisters" know that having babies out of wedlock was always a mistake, a sure way to truncate one's hopes and dreams. "You want something to love?" she asked the girls in her Big Sisters group. "Tell me and I'll get you a puppy!"

Nineteen eighty-six was turning out to be a banner year for Oprah. Her acting career continued with a role in the film adaptation of Richard Wright's *Native Son*, the story of twenty-year-old Bigger Thomas, an African American struggling to survive Chicago's South Side ghetto in the 1930s. Oprah played Bigger's mother, and since the role was small and the movie was being filmed in Chicago, there was no problem taking time off from her television show. When the movie came out, it did not do particularly well at the box office, but once again Oprah garnered good notices for her acting.

With all that was happening in Oprah's life, she felt it was important to keep her friends close. In the spring of 1986, she went Hyannis, Massachusetts, to attend the wedding of Maria Shriver to action-film star Arnold Schwarzenegger. Maria asked Oprah to recite Elizabeth Barrett Browning's poem beginning "How do I love thee?" Dining on lobster and champagne, mingling with Maria's family—the powerful Kennedys, including former First Lady Jacqueline Kennedy Onassis—Oprah must have felt she'd come a long way from feeding chickens on her grandmother's farm.

Oprah was also in constant contact with her best friend from Baltimore, Gayle King. The two talked on the phone every night. "We laugh," Oprah once wrote about the relationship. "She has helped me through demotions, near firings, sexual harassment, and the twisted, messed-up relationships of my twenties." Now that there were more good times than bad, Gayle was also there. "For every new level of success I achieve, you can believe she's somewhere in the background, cheering louder and smiling broader than anyone else."

Although Oprah did not make new friends easily, perhaps wary that people would like her for what she could do for them rather than for who she was, someone came into her life during the early years of her television show who would be more than a friend. Poet, writer, and educator Maya Angelou, author of one of Oprah's favorite books, *I Know Why the Caged Bird Sings*, became a mentor to her. Oprah has called Angelou her spiritual mother.

When she first met Angelou, the bond was immediate, with the two talking as if they had known each other forever. Perhaps that was because their lives were marked by important parallels. Both had been raised in the South by their grandmothers and acquired a sense of self-worth as children from speaking in churches, the congregation nodding approvingly and tossing "amen"s at them as they delivered their "little pieces." Perhaps most importantly, both women knew the pain and shame of being raped as girls.

Angelou's presence in Oprah's life gave her a stability that she was never able to get from her own mother. Going to Angelou's North Carolina home, spending time talking with her, hearing her stories, and eating the down-home cooking Angelou loved preparing was like a homecoming. Oprah has said that being in Angelou's presence is like a warm bath after an exhausting day.

There were many exhausting days and nights for Oprah as the syndication deal with King World, brokered by her manager Jeff Jacobs, went into effect, and the show prepared to go national in the fall of 1986. Primed by magazine and newspaper articles, America was eager to see Ms. Winfrey on the small screen, especially after getting to know her at the movies.

Oprah has said that she was confident her new syndicated show would be successful, but she did wonder what it all meant. She wrote in her diary at midnight, the night before her show went national, "I keep wondering how my life will change. If it will change. And what this all means. Why have I been so blessed? Maybe going national was to help me realize that I have important work or that this work is important. Which is it? And I vacillate between letting this be the most spectacular moment ever and getting goose bumps tomorrow or trying to treat it as an ordinary show. I think I'll wind up doing a little bit of both. But I just want to acknowledge to the universe right now to God and all his glory my praise and thanksgiving for this experience."

The shows that Oprah did in her first week of national syndication were typical of talk-show fare at the time, with an accent on the sensational. Her first show was "How to Catch a Man," followed by a show on squabbling families. As the years passed, Oprah would become dissatisfied with this type of programming, but for now, it seemed to be what the television audience wanted.

Yet even in the beginning of her national show, Oprah wanted to do programs that made people think, and not just about their personal lives. In the early years, she felt it was part of her responsibility as a minority to bring issues of racism to the forefront of the nation's consciousness. In 1987, she read in the newspapers about Forsyth County, Georgia, a place where no blacks had lived since 1912, when three young black men were accused of raping a white woman. There was a trial, but the outcome was preordained; the defendants were found guilty and hanged. The rest of the African American residents were warned to leave or be lynched.

Then, seventy-five years later, on Martin Luther King Jr.'s birthday, thousands marched on Forsyth County in protest, and there were racial confrontations. Oprah and her staff decided they would go to Forsyth County to do a show. She went not to confront or argue, but simply to find out why twenty years after the Civil Rights Act, this community still did not allow African Americans to live among them. The show was insistent that only white residents be members of the audience, despite pressure from civil-rights groups that were marching outside. But Oprah wanted to hear what the people—white people— actually living in Forsyth County had to say for themselves. The conversation ranged from conciliatory to confrontational, even hostile, as the residents tried to explain their positions to a black woman who fit none of the preconceived notions many in the audience expressed about African Americans. It made for riveting television.

AIDS was another topic Oprah met head-on in 1987, a time when fear—and misinformation—about the disease was so widespread that people thought you could catch it from someone's tears. In Williamson, West Virginia, a young man with AIDS went swimming in a town pool. Many of the citizens were outraged, assuming that he had put the other swimmers in danger. Oprah had a town meeting–style show, which featured the AIDS victim as well as the men and women of Williamson. A few were sympathetic, most were angry, and many vented their feelings. A public-health official tried to reassure the audience that swimming in a pool was not the way AIDS was transmitted, but most people wanted an ironclad guarantee. One furious man said that all people with AIDS should be moved to reservations "like the Indians."

Although Oprah found these statements personally repugnant, she also understood that the audience members were coming from a place of fear. By doing this show, she wanted to put a human face on AIDS and to get the facts out. In later years, AIDS would touch her personally when friends and family members died of the disease. She would continue to keep AIDS sufferers as a cornerstone of her concerns, especially the women and children of Africa, who did not have access to the medicines that would become available to patients in developed countries like the United States.

Programs on controversial topics gave *The Oprah Winfrey Show* credibility in the eyes of viewers and brought more visibility and influence to Oprah personally. In fact, she was a phenomenon, her success across the country as complete as it had been in Chicago. Oprah had wondered in her diary how national syndication would change her life; the answer turned out to be: in every way possible.

After the show went national, it became a slicker, more polished production. During her earliest days in Chicago, the staff had been small, only six people, and their space had been so cramped that Oprah had to share an office. Her very first months, when the show was still called *A.M. Chicago*, it had no real system for getting a studio audience, so staff members would go outside on busy State Street and cajole shoppers to come inside and watch the show by offering them coffee and doughnuts. "I was the one who would go pick up the doughnuts before the show," Oprah noted.

Those days were over. The show was now bringing in big advertising dollars for the TV stations, and when the money started rolling in from her syndication deal, Oprah could hardly believe the amounts she was seeing. The teenager who wanted to be a "spendin' fool" if she had a million dollars soon found herself holding a check for a million dollars right in her hand. The day it arrived, she and Gayle, who was visiting from Baltimore, ran around and around the apartment with it, hooting and hollering. After just the first year of syndication, Oprah was estimated to have received millions more.

Two years after the show went national, her manager, Jeff Jacobs, came up with a new way for Oprah to increase her control over the show. He worked out a deal where Oprah would part company with ABC, except for their right to have her program on their affiliate stations across the country, giving them a tremendous daytime TV advantage. She would own the show, and it would continue to be syndicated by King World.

Leaving ABC meant that Oprah needed a new studio, and Jacobs thought he had found just the place. In a desolate area, just west of downtown Chicago, were several dilapidated buildings originally used in the 1920s as movie studios. He thought they could be purchased and refurbished for about $20 million, a huge sum, but not outrageous considering that the facility would not just be used for *The Oprah Winfrey Show* but for other productions that would be made there. Oprah was already buying the rights to books she wanted to turn into TV movies, such as Zora Neale Hurston's *Their Eyes Were Watching God*, another story of a black woman's struggle.

"Had I not taken ownership of the show, I would not have pursued the idea of having my own studio," Oprah said once the deal was complete. "One thing would not have worked out without the other. I did this to really expand the areas I wanted and take over the show to create more time for me to do features and TV specials."

There had been only two women in the history of

film to own their own studios. One was silent-movie star Mary Pickford. The other was actress and comedienne Lucille Ball. That made Oprah the third, and also the first African American to own a studio. The facility was large, with three studios, office space, workshops for carpentry and painting, screening rooms, and parking. Even Oprah was impressed with her own success. "This is really something," she said as Harpo Studios was being launched. "I think this is the 'big time' I've heard so much about."

Her studio wasn't the only big land purchase Oprah made in 1988. Around the same time, she bought a farm in an area of Indiana called Rolling Prairie. A farm it may have been called, but it was nothing like the hardscrabble dirt farm where she'd spent her early years in Mississippi. With a stone castle-like building at its center, a riding stable, a tennis court, and a swimming pool, the property was more reminiscent of a country estate. About an hour from Chicago, it was a place where she could relax with Stedman and run around with her beloved cocker spaniels, Solomon and Sophie.

When she was working, Oprah lived in a sprawling

penthouse apartment in one of the city's prestigious buildings. Located off the "Magnificent Mile," the nickname of the city's fashionable shopping area, Oprah's condominium had fabulous views of the city skyline. She was on top of the world literally as well as figuratively.

The television show *60 Minutes* interviewed Oprah the year her show went into syndication. The host, Mike Wallace, called her "a sudden, soaring success," and seemed almost surprised that someone from her background had come so far so fast. Oprah was not very surprised, because she understood the reason for her success: "I communicate with all these people because I think I'm every woman. I've had every malady, and I've been on every diet, and I've had men who have done me wrong, honey." She could relate to her audiences, and they saw themselves reflected back to her.

She also told Wallace that even though her show was a success, it did not define her. "I think we are defined by the way we treat ourselves and the way we treat other people."

Eight

TOM CRUISE. BARBRA STREISAND. Halle Berry. Oprah Winfrey has interviewed the biggest stars in the world. Some were her role models, like Barbara Walters. Others—John Travolta, Tina Turner, Jamie Foxx—became her friends.

Yet no matter how rich and popular Oprah became— and by the 1990s she was one of the richest and most popular women in the country—she still had issues she struggled with. Like every person, there were things in her past that caused pain in the present.

An ongoing problem was her weight. Watching television clips of Oprah over the years, it is startling to see how her weight varies from season to season. Sometimes she seems almost petite; at other times she looks seriously overweight. Oprah was in the spotlight, and that light was often shining on how she looked and how much she weighed. There seemed to be a magazine or tabloid article for every pound she lost—and gained.

In the summer of 1988, Oprah decided she needed to try something drastic; her weight had ballooned 70 pounds since her Chicago debut, and she was now at 212 pounds. She went on a liquid diet called Opti-fast, and for almost four and half months she ate nothing, nothing at all, sipping only her liquid diet. The show was on hiatus—its summer break—and the rumor mill was churning out stories in the tabloids that Oprah was losing weight, but no one knew the details. Her goal was to get herself back into a pair of skinny jeans that she had optimistically saved since her Baltimore days.

Sure enough, in November, Oprah came onstage dressed in a tight black turtleneck and those skin-hugging jeans, pulling a little red wagon heaped high with sixty-seven pounds of fat, the amount of weight that she had lost. Oprah tried to lift the bagged fat and couldn't. She remarked that it seemed impossible to believe that she was unable to pick up the same amount of fat that she had carried around on her body.

On November 16, 1988, Oprah pulled a little red wagon onto her stage piled with sixty-seven pounds of animal fat, representing her weight loss.

"The Fat in the Wagon" show, as it was called, would turn out to be the highest rated Oprah show ever. But the weight loss itself was not such a success. Unaware that, by being on such a stringent diet, she had, in effect, been starving herself, Oprah had messed up her metabolism so badly that every morsel she ate after the diet turned immediately into weight gain. She remembers, "I was the smallest I had ever been for that show and for several hours afterward. After that, I started regaining the weight, and by two days later I couldn't fit into those jeans anymore."

Just months later she was doing a show about regaining weight. Eventually, she would regain all the weight she had lost and add more. Oprah continued to go up and down over the years, a classic "yo-yo" dieter. But in some ironic way, her weight battle only endeared her to her audience, especially because she spoke so honestly about what she was going through. They could relate to her stories, like the one she told about the first time she was dieting seriously back in Baltimore and got a craving. Since she had cleared the house of food, there was nothing to eat but frozen hot-dog buns and syrup. "So I put the syrup over those frozen hot-dog buns, and I ate 'em! I did that!" Her audience, over-whelmingly women, laughed with her, identified with her, and sympathized.

Coming from a place of honesty was very important to Oprah, and when it came to weight matters, she real-ized early on that lying would be ridiculous since every-one could see what was happening anyway. Truthful about how the pounds impacted her life—"There are days when I wake up with all the wonderful things happening in my life . . . and I still hate myself because of my weight"—she also admitted that the tabloid stories about her were painful, especially when jealous people would try to use her weight against her. One example was the ugly rumor about Stedman cheating on her not with a woman but with a man. Oprah made the point that if she had been thin, no one would have questioned why a man as handsome as Graham would be satisfied with her.

Over the years, many *Oprah* shows were about dieting, and the topics ranged from the diets she had tried (the Egg-and-Weenie diet, the Think-Yourself-Thin diet) to prejudice against fat people. It was as if Oprah was trying to understand her own weight issues by exploring them in various ways on her television program.

Yet no matter how much she discussed the issue, it wasn't even close to being resolved. By 1992, Oprah's weight was at an all-time high—237 pounds. She had just won her third Daytime Emmy Award for Outstanding Talk Show Host, but in an evening reminiscent of Oscar night, what should have been a triumph was instead a nightmare. She was "mortified," at her size and that she had to "waddle" up to get her award. "I felt like such a loser, like I'd lost control of my life. I was the fattest woman in the room."

Determined to get that control back, Oprah was once again ready to get serious about her weight. Immediately after the Emmys, she went to a spa in Telluride, Colorado, where she met Bob Greene, a personal trainer who started her on an exercise program. Then she hired a chef, Rosie Daley, who prepared healthy, low-fat meals for her. Together Oprah and Rosie wrote a book called *In the Kitchen with Rosie*, which was a best seller. But having someone monitor her meals didn't solve her issues with weight because she was not yet getting to the root of her problems. It wasn't so much what Oprah was eating, but what was eating her.

Real progress began when she hired Bob Greene to come to Chicago to work with her exclusively. His first success was to get the notoriously exercise-phobic Oprah on track—literally. Greene soon had Oprah walking with the goal of moving up to jogging and eventually competing in a marathon. To Oprah, running for twenty-six miles, the length of a marathon, seemed an impossibility. She wasn't sure she could run one mile, nor did she particularly want to. Nevertheless, in 1994, with Greene monitoring her progress, she began training, running ten to twelve miles some mornings before taping her show. On the weekends, she would kick it up a notch and run fifteen miles or more.

The strenuous training paid off. In October, she went to Washington, D.C., for the Marine Marathon, one runner among fifteen thousand. It was pouring rain on race day, but Oprah was not deterred by the weather—nor by the two *National Enquirer* reporters who insisted on running the race alongside her to get the scoop up close and personal.

The most difficult part of any marathon usually comes around mile twenty-one, when runners feel like they have to push through a wall of pain. Oprah had to make that push while wading through the water; it was raining so hard, her gray running clothes and cap were soaked through. Once she made it past the twenty-one-mile mark, Oprah knew that she would finish the race, crying when the finish line came into view. Stating that the cheers of the supportive crowd helped carry her through, she clocked in at just under four hours and thirty minutes. Running a marathon was a huge accomplishment. Oprah said it was one of the most difficult things she had ever done, and it gave her one of the best feelings she ever had. She added frankly that running one marathon was enough, and she had no desire ever to do it again.

Bob Greene was incredibly proud of Oprah, noting that she had worked as hard as any athlete he had ever seen. Now it was time for her to really get to the root of her weight problems. Greene was the first person who made Oprah see that she was using food as medication to calm herself down. When she was nervous or upset, she would think to herself, "I gotta eat,

I gotta eat. I gotta eat." Yet when Greene tried to tell her that the reason she ate was because she didn't love herself, she was indignant. "'I'm Oprah Winfrey. I love myself,' I told him. 'I've read every book about loving yourself.'"

After the marathon, her weight still fluctuated, although not so wildly. She even wrote a book with Greene, titled *Make the Connection*. It was about taking charge of your life and changing the way you think about food. It was published in 1996, and it was a huge seller, yet years later Oprah admitted that even while writing it, she never entirely made the connection herself. "I would ask Bob, 'Now what's the connection again?' And he would tell me, 'It's loving yourself and feeling that you are worthy of taking care of yourself.' Then two weeks later I'd say, 'Now what is that connection again?' It was only in 2002 or '03 that I really fully understood."

What Oprah finally learned was that diets don't work because the relationship an overweight person has with food is more about emotions than hunger. In her case, she was convinced the belief that she was destined to be overweight came in her teen years. She distinctly remembers getting off the scale one day and her father telling her, "Girl, no need to keep weighing yourself. You're a nice size now, but you're going to be a heavy girl. All of your people are heavy. Look at your mama, your aunt, your grandmother. Your whole family's heavy. No way around it." Oprah said the comment "undermined all my greatest efforts" to deal with her weight. When she finally realized that this unconscious belief, coupled with the leftover feelings from her abuse and her high stress level as she gained more prominence, were behind her weight issues, she at last "made the connection."

Despite all the misery being overweight had caused her, Oprah later said that she wouldn't have traded the experience for anything. Going through the pain and the sorrow that being overweight brought had helped her to become more empathetic and more understanding of the different sorts of pain that other people go through.

Another of Oprah's major struggles centered on her relationship with her family. Although she had done numerous shows on family dynamics and how to improve them, her own family life was rocky.

Grandma Hattie was long dead, and Oprah's relationship with her mother had been strained since she left Milwaukee as a rebellious fourteen-year-old. Although she was in close contact with her father and Zelma, she had barely seen her mother and her half-sister and half-brother, Patricia and Jeffrey, until her television career took off. Once she was financially able, she helped out her mother and siblings, but they were never close.

Patricia and Jeffrey had serious problems of their own. Patricia dealt with a drug addiction so severe she was sometimes unable to take care of her two daughters, Chrishaunda and Alicia, even though Oprah would send her money to help support the girls. Oprah was so furious when her eldest niece called to tell her that there was no food in the house that she cut Patricia off, sending the girls to their grandmother Vernita's house so that they could be taken care of. Patricia would eventually go to a drug-rehabilitation center, though that did not solve all her problems. She would die in 2003.

Jeffrey, the little brother Oprah barely knew, was in even worse shape—he was dying of AIDS. A gay man who was also a drug user, Jeffrey had contracted the disease either through a sexual partner or his drug use. Oprah had tried to help him financially, as well, only to see him use the money for drugs. In 1989, when he was just twenty-nine years old, Jeffrey Lee died at the Green Tree Health Care Center in Milwaukee. Oprah issued a statement that said: "My family, like thousands of others throughout the world, grieves not just for the death of one young man, but for the many unfulfilled dreams and accomplishments that society has been denied because of AIDS."

Then, in 1992, Oprah experienced a vicious betrayal when Patricia sold the story of Oprah's pregnancy and the death of her premature baby boy to a tabloid newspaper, *The National Enquirer*. Oprah knew that as such a public figure, she would probably have to share that detail of her life at some point, but she had not been ready to face it yet. Later she said that she wanted to wait until she had found a way to make the experience an object lesson for young girls who also had to deal with an unwanted pregnancy.

With the news out, Oprah went on record with the Sunday newspaper supplement *Parade*, and explained why she had kept the incident hidden. "The experience was the most emotional, confusing, and traumatic of my young life."

Later she told another magazine, *Ebony*, how she had learned about her sister's betrayal. She was shooting the television show *The Women of Brewster Place* at her Harpo Studios when Stedman came to tell her about the article before she saw it on the newsstands or heard about it from someone else. "I went home and got in bed and cried," she remembered. "I thought the whole world was going to hate me when they found out. And to have my sister tell it!"

Stedman, too, was crying when he gave her the paper, saying, "You don't deserve this." Oprah was especially touched that Stedman made it his business to confront her sister and tell Patricia how angry he was about her actions.

Whether Patricia had sold the story out of jealousy or simply for the money is impossible for outsiders to know, but Oprah didn't speak to her sister for two years. Finally she called a family meeting at her farm in Indiana, inviting her mother, sister, and several other women relatives. With Oprah playing the role of therapist, they discussed what had happened, and Oprah was able to forgive—if not forget. She felt deeply that since she was on television talking about forgiveness so often, she would be a hypocrite if she couldn't find some way to forgive her sister.

Living a life that had been filled with such highs and lows, Oprah decided that the next big thing on her "to do" list was to write a book about her experiences and the lessons that she had learned. Publishers jumped at the chance to be the one to publish the autobiography of Oprah Winfrey. Knopf eventually won the rights, and Oprah worked diligently on the book. The announcement about its forthcoming publication was made with great fanfare at the American Booksellers Convention in 1993 with Oprah announcing that she had written a book that would change people's lives. Booksellers from around the country were deliriously happy. If anyone could get customers into their stores, it was Oprah. Her autobiography was a guaranteed best seller.

The booksellers might have been thrilled, but the moment Oprah stepped off the stage, she was miserable. "I should have been exhilarated, but I was feeling, 'Oh God, what have I done?' I've said I've written this great book, but I don't think what I've promised is what I have."

She thought she had done "a masterful job" of chronicling her life, but a traditional autobiography, full of names and dates, was not what she had set out to write. "I wanted to write a book that would empower people." Her hope was to write a book about her own life that would have relevance to others. After showing the book to Stedman and other close friends, she realized that she hadn't met the challenge she had set for herself.

Yet the people-pleasing side of Oprah, the part that was fearful others might get mad at her, was afraid to tell her publishers that she wanted to withdraw the book. What would people think if she didn't meet her obligation? More importantly, how would they feel about *her*? Still the little voice inside Oprah's head, the one that she relied upon to make the best decisions, was telling her not to publish.

After agonizing over the decision, Oprah informed her editor at Knopf that she was withdrawing the manuscript. Were people disappointed? Yes. But Oprah was able to withstand the upset and anger because she was doing what she knew was the right thing.

Ironically, the unpublished book did turn out to be important and relevant—to her. As she saw her life spread out before her in black and white, it became clear to Oprah that much of the pain she had experienced was a result of worrying about what people would think of her. That was why she suffered alone when she knew she was pregnant, and in part why she kept on the weight. Throughout the 1990s and beyond, Oprah made serious inroads into her personal problems, not giving up until she found solutions that really worked. Often she made the decision to deal with them in public, either on her show or in the press. That was tough, but Oprah realized that by sharing her struggles, she was helping her viewers fight their own demons.

Nine

IT WAS NICKNAMED "Trash TV." By the 1990s, after the national success of programs like those of Phil Donahue and Oprah Winfrey, more and more talk shows got in the game—and the goal was to rope in viewers. One surefire way to get people to tune in was to shock them with sordid subjects, weird people, and lots of yelling, fighting, and crying. The most notorious of the Trash TV broadcasters—who included Sally Jessy Raphael, Geraldo Rivera, and Ricki Lake—was Jerry Springer. Springer's show was punctuated by brawls, near-nakedness, and bleep-out language. TV critics were quick to condemn shows with titles like "Hairdresser Horror Stories," "Man-Stealing Relatives," and "Women Who Are Allergic to Their Husbands." But these were not segments on Springer's daily talk show. They were on *Oprah*. Even though Oprah always tried to balance her lighter programming with shows of significance, she was not immune to trying to keep up with her trashier counterparts.

After a while, Oprah became unhappy with the direction that her shows were taking. In a 1994 interview with the magazine *Entertainment Weekly*, she noted, "I've been guilty of doing Trash TV and not even thinking it was trash. I don't want to do it anymore. But for the past ten years, we've been leading the way for doing issues that change people's lives. So I'm irritated and frustrated at being lumped in with those other shows."

She began accentuating the positive in her programs. In 1996 and 1997, the theme of many of the shows was "Make the Connection," keyed to the title of the book she had written with Bob Greene and dealing with the effect that emotions and unresolved problems had on people's lives.

In 1998, Oprah went a step further, and she dubbed her new season, "Change Your Life TV." "I want to use television as the medium for communicating to people a way to better their lives," Oprah told *TV*

Guide. This translated into shows with family, financial, and relationship experts. Parts of some of the shows were dedicated to "Remembering Your Spirit," aimed at helping readers get in touch with the spiritual side of themselves.

To the surprise of no one, including Oprah, when her shows became more uplifting, her ratings went down. She had, in fact, predicted just that in 1995, when she first started to make a concerted effort to distance herself from the sleaze pack. "We've grown in the past ten years. And I want the shows to reflect that growth—even if our ratings go in the tank."

To add insult to injury, after losing viewers who wanted the more titillating shows, she got hit with criticism from those who thought Oprah was getting too preachy and goody-goody. Some TV critics began writing about her bottomless ego and New Age nuttiness. But Oprah was not the people pleaser she once had been, and the criticism didn't seem to bother her. The older she got and the more demons she faced, the stronger she became, especially when it came to knowing what was right for her. One important instance was how she dealt with her childhood abuse.

During a show in 1990, Oprah was interviewing a woman who had developed multiple personalities to mentally protect herself from the brutal abuse she experienced as a child. As the woman spoke, Oprah could feel the tears welling up. The recounting of the abuse brought Oprah in touch with her own abuse, and the feelings were powerful. "So it happened on the air, as so many things happen for me. It happened on the air in the middle of someone else's experience. I thought I was going to have a breakdown." Oprah repeatedly told her director to stop filming, but her producer insisted that the show continue.

As she tried to get through the interview, Oprah realized just how much being molested had affected her and still affected her. In ways she hadn't even understood, she blamed herself for her abuse. "I would . . . speak to people and say, 'Oh, the child's never to blame. You're never responsible for the molestation in your life.' I still believed I was responsible somehow. That I was a bad girl."

Oprah decided that she would become an advocate for abused children. In 1991, she initiated a national campaign against child abuse. Not only did she want to raise awareness of the subject, she was determined to back legislation that would help make children safer. She was spurred on by the case of a Chicago girl, raped and murdered, whose body was found in Lake Michigan. The child's murderer had previously been convicted for other sex crimes. Oprah hired former Illinois governor Jim Thompson, now a lawyer in private practice, to draft a federal child protection law that would create a data bank with information about convicted child abusers.

Senator Joseph Biden of Delaware introduced the legislation into Congress, and Oprah testified about the bill before the Senate Judiciary Committee, which Senator Biden chaired. The bill specifically asked for funding for an FBI database to be used by schools and child-care agencies to check the backgrounds of employees.

Although the legislation gained the support of many legislators, when it came time to be voted upon, it was attached to a crime bill that was opposed by the powerful National Rifle Association, among others. The bill almost passed but ultimately did not receive enough votes. Oprah was not happy. "Almost," she said, "does not save a child."

Still she didn't allow her crusade to end there. In 1992, she hosted a TV documentary titled *Scared Silent: Exposing Child Abuse*. For the first time in television history, a non-news show aired simultaneously on all of the networks—ABC, CBS, NBC, and PBS.

"I'm Oprah Winfrey, and like millions of other Americans, I'm a survivor of child abuse." That was how the show began. It focused on sexual, physical, and mental abuse, and after it aired, the child-abuse hotline with which it was affiliated received more than 112,000 phone calls. The hotline director noted that the response exceeded anyone's expectations. The documentary brought new life to the legislation that Oprah had tried to help pass a few years earlier. In 1993, the Congress passed the National Child Protection Act, but it was dubbed the Oprah Winfrey Law. Oprah was in Washington, D.C., looking on when President Bill Clinton signed it into law.

Over the years, Oprah continued her work against child molestation with television shows on the topic and in her public writings. In 2005, with several particularly horrific cases of child abduction and murder in the news, Oprah decided to once again put all the power of her public persona into her crusade.

Standing alone on her set, she made her intention clear. "Enough is enough. With every breath in my body, whatever it takes, with your support, we are going to move heaven and earth to stop a sickness that is the definition of evil that's been going on for far too long." Putting up a $100,000 reward for each capture, Oprah showed photographs of child predators on her show and on her Web site, and asked her viewers to help find them. Within a matter of weeks, several predators were found and arrested. She was grateful for every molester she and her audience were able to get off the street.

The crusade against child abuse was one Oprah was happy to lead, but in 1996 she found herself in the middle of a fight that shocked and dismayed her. That year, she did a show on mad cow disease, following a furor in the press about several British cases of Creutzfeldt-Jakob disease, the human variant of mad cow, which can occur decades after a person has eaten diseased meat. Oprah had a guest who discussed how cows in the United States were not being properly screened. "He has just stopped me cold from eating another burger," Oprah exclaimed.

The power of Oprah Winfrey was demonstrated quickly. Beef prices fell precipitously, and Texas ranchers were furious. A group of them sued Oprah for $12 million, claiming that the show "carefully and maliciously edited statements that were designed to hype ratings at the expense of the American cattle industry." The suit claimed that Oprah was responsible for the drop in beef prices, but Oprah's lawyers countered by saying that the law under which she was being sued was an infringement of the First Amendment, which guarantees the right to free speech. The trial was set for January 21, 1998, and was scheduled to take place in Texas.

Oprah took the show to Amarillo, Texas, for the length of the trial. She didn't have much choice— she was contracted for two hundred shows a year. The trial lasted for six weeks, and they were difficult ones for Oprah. She spent her days in the courtroom, and at night she did her television shows. Her staff put together a small makeshift studio in Amarillo, where local audiences could come to see the show. Trailers were fixed up for dressing rooms, with others as cramped spaces to do Oprah's hair and makeup. Trying to make herself at home, she filled her living and working spaces with pictures of friends and family; her beloved cocker spaniel Sophie accompanied her on the trip.

It was during this trial that Oprah met someone who was to become her protégé and eventually launch his own television show: Philip McGraw, now known to millions as Dr. Phil. As one of the founders of a company called Courtroom Sciences, Inc., Dr. Phil helped Oprah prepare for the trial by analyzing jurors, examining relevant laws, and conducting mock trials, all to help her lawyers prepare their best defense. Oprah saw something in the no-nonsense psychologist that led her to believe his "tell it like it is" style would appeal to her audience. After the trial was over, she gave the advice guru his own regular spot on her show.

The experience was harder to go through than she had imagined, and the worst moment came when she was being cross-examined by the cattlemen's lawyer. Oprah remembered sitting on the stand and the lawyer standing so close to her, he was spitting in her face as he called her a liar and a manipulator. But in the midst of that cross-examination, Oprah said she had one of what she calls her "lightbulb moments," where she sees something in a new way. As the lawyer lit into her, Oprah realized that "the things that happen outside you don't define you." She says the moment she had that realization, she felt like no matter the outcome of the trial, she had already won.

As she did with so many things that happened to her, Oprah tried to extend the life lesson to her viewers. "Everyone has a trial," she said later, "but you have to say, 'I'm not my disease, no I'm not the beatings.' You have to stand inside of yourself, and know that you are not the devastation that is happening to you. *This* is who I am."

Even though Oprah had made peace with the experience, she was still thrilled that when the verdict from the jury came down, she was found not guilty. Striding out of the courthouse, a huge smile on her face, Oprah faced the cameras and said, "Free speech not only lives, it rocks!"

Sued by a group of Texas ranchers who claimed she had defamed the beef industry, Oprah was ecstatic when the jury found her innocent in 1998.

As Oprah tried to distance herself more and more from Trash TV, she found different ways to make her show part of the solution, rather than part of the problem. Sometimes the smallest things gave

Oprah big ideas. That was the case with her Angel Network, which invites viewers to help improve the lives of others. The idea sprouted when Oprah heard about a little girl named Norah who started collecting pennies for charity from friends and neighbors and wound up with thousands of dollars. If a child could collect that much money, Oprah thought, how much could her audience put in what she was calling "the world's largest piggy bank"? Asking viewers for their spare change, she hoped to provide scholarships for fifty needy students, one from every state in the union.

This was not the first time Oprah had been involved in providing scholarships to those in need. Back in 1987, Oprah had decided to fulfill a promise she had made to her father, Vernon, to finally finish up the senior project she had left undone at Tennessee State University when she moved to Baltimore. After she completed the requirements, the university asked her to give the commencement address when she received her diploma along with the rest of the graduating class. In her speech, Oprah announced that she was endowing ten scholarships to the school in honor of her father, who had always encouraged her to pursue an education, telling her it was the keystone to a successful future.

The response to the world's largest piggy bank was overwhelming. Even First Lady Hillary Clinton came on Oprah's show with a piggy bank her own family had been dropping coins into. In ten months, more than one million dollars was collected, and each of the fifty students was provided with a $25,000 scholarship.

At the same time, Oprah was using the Angel Network to build homes with Habitat for Humanity for those in need. Two hundred homes were built all over the country from Anchorage, Alaska, to Dallas, Texas.

In 1998, the Angel Network officially became a public charity formed to encourage people to make a difference in the lives of others. Oprah's Angel Network supports charitable projects and provides grants to nonprofit organizations around the world. In the wake of the Hurricane Katrina disaster, it offered ways for viewers to help build houses and furnish them for those left homeless. The Angel Network is also building schools in countries throughout the world, including some in Asia, South America, and Africa. By 2005, the Angel Network had raised more than $27 million. One hundred percent of the funds raised goes to charity.

Ten

MOST PEOPLE FIND something that they're good at and stick to it. Oprah Winfrey is interested in many different areas of the arts and communication, and she has pursued them all. Movies, cable television, book and magazine publishing, theater—over the years, Oprah was to become successful in all of those venues.

Hosting a talk show that she could use as a forum to showcase her ideas and inspire others was what Oprah felt most comfortable and useful doing, but she always held on to the dream of being an actress. That dream came true when she appeared in *The Color Purple* and *Native Son*, but Oprah knew that it would be difficult to continue finding roles that she was suited for. After all, most Hollywood actresses are young, white, and thin. She was over thirty when she got the role of Sofia, she was never going to be white, and she was thin only sporadically. Oprah realized early on that if she was going to stay involved in the movie business, she was going to have to carve out that career for herself.

The first step had been creating Harpo Studios, a site where she would tape her television show and develop other projects that she might act in, produce, or both. In 1988, the year she became the youngest recipient of the prestigious Broadcaster of the Year Award, she began production on a miniseries titled *The Women of Brewster Place*, adapted from a novel by Gloria Naylor. It is the story of seven African American women who live in a tenement building, trying against all odds to raise their families. These were characters whom Oprah understood: women like her mother and others she had known in her Milwaukee neighborhood, who struggled every day to keep their families physically and emotionally intact despite tough circumstances. The movie also showed the neighborhood as a place full of life and dreams, where friends took care of friends, watching each other's backs. With her hair dyed gray, Oprah played one of the neighborhood women, along with actresses Cicely Tyson and Robin Givens.

As with *The Color Purple*, the show was not without controversy when it came to its treatment of African American men. The National Association for the Advancement of Colored People (NAACP) asked to look at the scripts before production started to see if some of the negative images of black men that were in Naylor's book were also going to be a part of the miniseries. Harpo Productions refused that request but did temper some of the male portrayals and made them more nuanced. Once again, Oprah's focus was to show the everyday lives of black women and how, in spite of myriad disappointments, they woke up each day and pushed forward again.

The miniseries got mixed reviews, but its ratings were high enough for ABC to ask for more episodes to spin off into a weekly series. Oprah threw herself into the project, but viewers had less interest in watching a weekly series, and after four episodes, *The Women of Brewster Place* was canceled. Nevertheless she returned to the subject of an African American mother trying to raise her children in the 1993 TV movie, based on a true story, *There Are No Children Here*. "We might be poor, but we ain't selling our souls to the devil today,"

Oprah says as LaJoe Rivers, a character in the story. Filming in part at Chicago's Henry Horner projects, where the book of the same name by Alex Kotlowitz was set, Oprah made sure that some of the residents were used as extras.

Several other projects that Harpo Studios produced from books that Oprah had optioned starred the Academy Award–winning actress Halle Berry. One was *The Wedding* (1998), about upper-class African Americans living on Martha's Vineyard in the 1950s. The TV movie explored issues of racial intermarriage. Then in 2005, Berry starred in another pet project of Oprah's, a TV-movie version of Zorah Neale Hurston's classic, *Their Eyes Were Watching God*.

Oprah had first read the book on a plane trip and cried throughout the journey as she became immersed in the life of Janie Crawford, a black woman living during the 1920s, who sought romantic and spiritual fulfillment despite the frowns of society. Oprah has said she was attracted to the book because "it was the greatest love story ever." Determined to bring the book to the screen, Oprah called Halle Berry the day after she won an Academy Award for her role in *Monster's*

Ball and asked her to play Janie, though she wasn't sure Berry would want do a television movie after winning an Oscar. But Berry was attracted to Hurston's story and its themes of love, community, and survival, which for her transcended color.

Although many people enjoyed the movie, those who had loved the book were ironically its biggest critics. They lamented the loss of the "blackness" they had found in the book: certain inauthentic accents, for example, and the erasure of particular African American struggles that had been smoothed over in an effort to make the story more universal.

The most important film project Oprah ever tackled, however, the one dearest to her heart, and the one that caused her the most pain, was *Beloved*, a film adaptation of a book by Nobel Prize–winning author Toni Morrison.

Beloved is the story of Sethe, a former slave living with her grown daughter in the years after emancipation. When a friend, Paul D, moves in with Sethe, he is astonished by the malevolent energy he feels in the house, though Sethe tells him it's not evil, just sad. It comes from the ghost of the child Sethe killed to save her from slavery. Soon the spirit of the child materializes in the form of a ghostly teenager who calls herself "Beloved."

Beloved was a story that even Toni Morrison doubted could be made into a movie. The book's structure is deliberately complex and labyrinthine as it moves through memory and imagination, back and forth in time, to deal with the painful, dehumanizing incidents that are at the heart of slavery. Yet the story resonated so deeply with Oprah that she was determined to bring Sethe's story to the screen.

She told a BBC interviewer, "It's a love story, it's all encompassing, it's a spiritual odyssey, it's a historical saga, and drama. It's one woman's quest to reconstruct her memories. . . . I think what Toni Morrison did is show what slavery felt like and not just what it looked like in the book *Beloved*."

Oprah was going to play Sethe herself, and to do so she immersed herself in the experience of slavery. While preparing for the role, she arranged a trip along a portion of the Underground Railroad, the route used by abolitionists to helps slaves escape to the North and to freedom. As she told the BBC, "I wanted to connect with what it felt like to be a slave wandering through the woods, making the way north to a life beyond slavery—a life where being free, at its most basic level, meant not having a master telling you what to do every minute." But the experience, even though it was just a reenactment, was much rougher than Oprah expected. Left alone in the Maryland woods, she felt tremendous fear as white men, playing the role of slave traders, tried to track her down.

"I became hysterical," Oprah admitted. "I went to the darkest place, and I saw the light. I thought, 'So this is where I come from.'"

After a long search for the right director, Oprah signed on acclaimed filmmaker Jonathan Demme. Filming began in 1997, ten years after Oprah had first read the book that she has said made her feel "ruined, overwhelmed, and redeemed, all at the same time."

She chronicled the evolution of the movie in a journal that she kept while filming; the journal was eventually published as a book, *Journey to Beloved*. As the book makes clear, the moviemaking process was intense. Oprah not only had to connect with Sethe's despair and hopelessness, she had to go to a place deep within herself to play scenes of rape and murder.

So completely did she lose herself in the role that at times she was frightened by her feelings. On days when she didn't know if she could bear to do one more scene of violence, she would light a candle and call out the names of real slaves, some of whose identity papers she had gathered, or she'd whisper her intention: "Today, I'm doing this for you, Big Annie." Danny Glover, the male lead in the movie, also became so emotionally involved that at one point he broke down. With tears streaming down his face, he told Oprah he felt surrounded by the spirits of the American slaves.

The movie premiered with much fanfare in 1998. It received solid critical acclaim, but audiences didn't want to see it. Despite a media blitz by Oprah that normally would have assured an easy success, people stayed away in droves. Those who did see the film were often bewildered by the structure and were disturbed by the graphic violence.

Oprah Winfrey was not used to failure, certainly not of this magnitude and of such a personal nature. She had called the film her baby, and it was as if the movie-

The movie Beloved, *based on Toni Morrison's book, was a project very close to Oprah's heart. She played the role of Sethe.*

going public had said, "This is one ugly, unappealing child." The insult hurt her to her core.

By her own admission, she was disheartened and depressed—and shocked—when the movie was beaten at the box office during its first weekend of release by even the low-budget horror flick *Bride of Chucky*. She couldn't get over it and couldn't explain it, even as the experience forced her to deal with her fear of failure. As she always did with the big events, she tried to figure out what life lesson she was supposed to be learning. But no matter how she struggled, she still couldn't reconcile her hopes for *Beloved* and the disappointment with the film's reception.

Then she made a call to Gary Zukav, a frequent guest on the show who wrote books about spiritual matters, in order to get his perspective on the situation. He asked her a simple question: What was your intention in making the movie?

Oprah had a ready answer for that. "To create a movie so powerful that it would allow people to feel, not just see, what it meant to overcome slavery and be able to love and to reconstruct a life," she responded.

"Well," Zukav replied, "you did that."

Finally Oprah had her lightbulb moment. She realized something she hadn't taken into account up until then: most people—black and white—didn't want to feel the intensity about slavery that she felt. "In that moment, I was willing to give up my expectation for box office numbers and just look at the work. I let go of my sadness," she said. "I started to feel grateful for every person who had seen the movie and felt moved and got in touch with their own humanity."

The larger lesson she learned was "to do your best, enjoy the journey, and let go of the outcome. Let it be."

It was no accident that Oprah kept finding movies she wanted to make out of books she loved. Of the many words that describe Oprah Winfrey, one of the most important would be "reader."

The list of books that have affected her is long, beginning with the stories of Lois Lenski, like *Strawberry Girl*, that she read when she was a young child. She has said that when she didn't have friends, she had books. One only has to remember that solitary girl sitting in the cafeteria of her high school in Milwaukee, reading, to know how much books meant to her. Unhappy and abused, Oprah let books take her away from the world she knew and open a window to another world, one of possibilities.

With this kind of bond to books, it was only natural that Oprah would want to bring her love of reading to her audience, and her vehicle was an on-air book club. The idea sprang from one of her producers, Alice McGee. For years, she and Oprah had traded books back and forth, discussed them, and brought others into their discussions. McGee came to Oprah and said, "Why don't we do this on the air?" At first, Oprah didn't quite get the idea. What? Have a book club on television? Well, yes.

The book club was a smashing success. Oprah and Alice decided that each month a new book would be introduced; the audience could read along, and then several members were invited to join the author of the selected book for dinner and a discussion. The criterion for a title being chosen was simple: Oprah had to love the book. The first book she picked was about the disappearance of a child, *The Deep End of the Ocean*, by Jacquelyn Mitchard.

Almost immediately, the face of the best-seller list was changed. Books that Oprah picked for her club, such as Wally Lamb's *She's Come Undone* and Isabel Allende's *Daughter of Fortune*, racked up spectacular sales, making Oprah a favorite of authors and publishers. But this success became a burden for the show as publishers pushed hard for their books to be a selection. In the years after 2000, she often picked classics like *East of Eden* and the works of William Faulkner to avoid the pressure of choosing new books; they, too, were met with positive receptions from audiences. It was the responses from the viewers that were most gratifying to Oprah. One woman admitted on the show that she had never before sat down and read a book. Someone else said that although she didn't always like the book-club selections, they would get her into bookstores, where she would find something else to read.

Despite the success of the book club, there was controversy on several occasions. In 2003, a bit of a literary squabble broke out when one author, Jonathan Franzen, was clearly unenthusiastic about his book *The Corrections* being chosen for the book club, feeling it was too literary for Oprah's audience. She promptly uninvited him to be on her show, since he was "uncomfortable."

Another, more serious incident occurred when it was learned that James Frey, the author of *A Million Little Pieces*, had distorted and changed some of the incidents in this memoir about his recovery from drug and alcohol abuse. Frey, for his part, said that although he had expanded some parts and compressed others, it was still his true story, but the literary community waited anxiously to see if Oprah would withdraw her support. In January 2006, she called in to *Larry King Live*, where Frey was a guest, and told the audience that although she was dismayed by the controversy, "the underlying message of the book still resonates with me and I know it resonates with the millions of people who read this book."

For once, Oprah's gut instinct was way off. People felt betrayed by Frey's decision to meld fact and fiction, and they were angry at Oprah for defending him. Then on a show later in January 2006, Oprah faced the cameras and said, "I made a mistake. I left the impression that the truth does not matter, and I am deeply sorry about that. That is not what I believe. . . . To everyone who has challenged me on this issue, you are absolutely right." Frey and his publisher, Nan A. Talese, were guests on the show that day, and Oprah gave them what can only be described as a public spanking, as she challenged their methods and his motives. The incident set off a firestorm as people across the country discussed the book, Oprah's responses, and even a writer's responsibility in writing memoirs.

Two other venues of entertainment felt Oprah's influence at the turn of the twenty-first century. In February of 2000, Harpo Productions went into partnership with Oxygen Media to develop a women's-interest cable network, Oxygen. It was a way to get more original programs on the air that would appeal to Oprah's core audience. Along with new programs, Oprah also extended *The Oprah Winfrey Show* with an hour on Oxygen called *Oprah After the Show*, an informal extension of the show, where audience members got to mix with the guests, asking questions and offering their opinions. In many ways it was a throwback to the early days of *The Oprah Winfrey Show*, when she often went into the audience with her microphone and the audience was a more integral part of the program.

But Oprah's greatest success in the new century was a magazine she launched in 2000, *O*. The Hearst Corporation, a huge publishing conglomerate, had come to see the influence Oprah had on the book world and thought that she could have an equally important role in magazine publishing.

The magazine got off to a rocky start when Hearst and Oprah had conflicting ideas of what the magazine would be like, but in the end, Oprah's vision of a magazine that would continue her TV show's crusade to inspire and empower women won out. She decided to call the magazine O, saying, "What I like about O is that it is simple and direct, and it is what a lot of my friends call me."

Before the magazine hit the newsstands, her editor in chief said that, "O reflects the close bond and inclusion which readers will experience with the magazine. O will be the women's personal growth guide for this new century, inspired by Oprah's unique vision."

Despite Oprah's popularity, starting a magazine is a risky business, and no one was sure how the magazine would be received when the first issue rolled off the presses in April of 2000. Not, that is, until the original print run of 850,000 copies sold out. Another 500,000 copies of the premier issue of O had to be rushed into print. The magazine turned out to have the most successful launch in publishing history. Within several years, its circulation base was more than two million readers.

At the fifth-year anniversary, the verdict was definitely in. O magazine was a critical and financial success. Beautifully produced on thick glossy paper, the magazine is filled with inspirational and self-help articles, recipes and book reviews, all designed to help readers "live their best life."

Oprah's fans loved it. For others, the magazine seemed to encompass everything they didn't like about her. They called it preachy, self-indulgent, New Agey, and egotistic. No one can deny, there's a lot of Oprah in each issue, including a monthly column, "What I Know for Sure," an interview, and a list of her favorite things. Some people particularly object to the magazine's cover: each issue features a glamorous photograph of Oprah, often doing something exciting like driving a sports car or riding a horse.

None of the criticism seems to bother her. Oprah felt very strongly that she wanted her relationship with the magazine to be hands-on, and she's pleased that it reflects her sensibility. As she once told her magazine staff, "I know to you guys the Oprah name is a brand, but for me it's my life . . . and the way I behave and everything I stand for." To make sure that her wishes are carried out in New York, where the magazine is produced, Oprah selected her best friend, Gayle King, to be the magazine's editor-at-large.

For the magazine's fifth anniversary, the editors put together a collection of Oprah's favorite "What I Know for Sure" columns. Readers will find the essence of Oprah in it. She writes about everything from the Golden Rule, which is the foundation of her beliefs; to the importance of being grateful, no matter what is happening; to her friendship with Gayle King and what it has meant to her. She also writes about the pain involved with the reception of *Beloved*.

In 2005, Oprah had the opportunity to become involved with another project that was dear to her heart. A musical version of *The Color Purple* was being brought to Broadway, and Oprah decided to participate, not as a performer, but as a producer. After she signed on, she met with the cast and told them, "There's an energy connected to what Alice [Walker, the author] first intended. When intention and energy combine . . . it's a holy moment for everybody involved, and I know you all feel it already, and now you will spread that energy to the world. I feel blessed to be a part of it."

Oprah's acting career had come full circle.

Eleven

OPRAH WINFREY BY the numbers:

The Oprah Winfrey Show is seen in 122 countries around the world: across Europe, throughout Africa, into Asia, from Iceland to the Western Sahara. Even in some of the most troubled spots in the world, like Iraq and Rwanda, people are still watching *Oprah.*

She is a billionaire and one of the most influential women in the world.

Two charities, the Oprah Winfrey Foundation and the Angel Network, are the venues through which she makes financial contributions to those in need. The Foundation, her private charity, focuses on empowering women and children. Through it, she has given more than $50 million of her own money.

Her television show has been the number one–rated talk show for more than twenty consecutive seasons.

The list of awards and honorary awards that Oprah has won is long, varied, and impressive. Besides forty Emmys for herself and her show, and her Oscar nomination, Oprah has won the National Freedom Award, was named one of *Time* magazine's 100 Most Influential People in the World, was awarded the National Book Foundation's Fiftieth Anniversary Gold Medal, received the Bob Hope Humanitarian Award, the Global Humanitarian Award from the United Nations, and the National Academy of Television Arts and Sciences Lifetime Achievement Award.

One of the most interesting things about Oprah Winfrey's life is how she manages two distinct aspects of it: fame and vast wealth, and her humanitarian impulses. Often, wealthy celebrities are known for their conspicuous consumption, and Oprah, who dreamed of being "a spendin' fool" when she was a teenager, is not opposed to spending her money on things she wants. She has, for example, made some very significant real-estate purchases. Besides her condo in Chicago, she owns land in Hawaii and a lavish home near Santa Barbara, California. The purchase of that seaside estate, which she bought in 2003 for $54 million, was reputed to be the largest private real-estate transaction in history.

Oprah also went all out for her fiftieth birthday in 2004. The celebration went on for a whole weekend, beginning with a birthday show taped at Harpo Studios. For days before the celebration, Oprah was exiled from the area as producers and staff went about planning the televised birthday extravaganza. Gayle King was the hostess; the audience was made up of friends and family, all of whom had received invitations in the form of a small book fashioned from exotic silk and studded with photographs from Oprah's life.

As the event began, Oprah, dressed in a flowing white blouse-and-pants outfit, walked out from the wings, bemused and feeling a little "out of sorts" because she was used to having complete control of the show. But her mood quickly turned to astonishment at the way the studio had been transformed. Seventeen floral designers and a crew of one hundred had prepared the site for the day, beautifying the space with thousands of rare orchids and roses. The flowers mingled with fabulous crystal chandeliers, made especially for the occasion, which hung from the ceiling.

The first surprise "gift" that came out of the wings

was Oprah's friend John Travolta, who toasted her with tears in his eyes saying that she "injected the spirit of life into our society." Other celebrities, such as Julia Roberts, Jennifer Lopez, Jennifer Aniston, Chris Rock, Tom Hanks, Jim Carrey, and Celine Dion, appeared via video to offer their own tributes. Tina Turner and Stevie Wonder sang two of Oprah's favorite songs. Nelson Mandela, former president of South Africa, made a moving speech in which he heralded her dedication to the welfare of the poor. Oprah was particularly touched by the tribute of actor Sidney Poitier. Seeing Poitier win an Academy Award for the movie *Lilies of the Field* in 1964 had been a powerful moment for the ten-year-old Oprah. Poitier was the first African American to win an Oscar for a leading role, and Oprah remembers thinking, "If he could do that, I wonder what I could do."

After the show, the guests were invited into another studio for a meal prepared by celebrity chef Wolfgang Puck that was topped off by a four-hundred-pound banana cake decorated with hand-painted portraits of Oprah and covered with beautiful handcrafted flowers, all edible.

And this was just the first of several parties that

continued throughout the weekend. Moving the celebration to the West Coast, Oprah hosted an all-female luncheon at the Bel Air Hotel in Los Angeles, and on Saturday evening, Oprah was the guest of honor at a formal dinner held at the home of her California neighbors. This event made her party at the studio look unassuming by comparison. At a cost of several million dollars, Oprah's friends had decorated their home with 100,000 orchids and had put a clear dance floor over their outdoor swimming pool. The celebrity guests—who included California governor Arnold Schwarzenegger and his wife Maria Shriver, Brad Pitt, Quincy Jones, and newswoman Diane Sawyer—were treated to a night of elegance and extravagance. For Oprah, it was a night to remember from the moment she and Stedman came through the door: "We walked in and there were about fifty violinists on the staircase, and then waiters all marched out—two hundred of them—and stood behind each person. It was the most glamorous, extravagant, fabulous thing anybody had ever seen!"

Everyone agreed the party was fabulous, but many people were turned off by the extravagance, which was called excessive by critics; even some fans thought there was something unseemly about such a conspicuous display of wealth. But Oprah wasn't apologizing, and she appreciated having such a birthday celebration. She laughingly tells a story about Stedman and how, after her fiftieth birthday parties, he said he no longer wanted to hear sad stories about how she was such a poor little girl that she ran around her grandmother's farm without shoes. Oprah had to admit that those years had more than been made up for.

Perhaps one reason Oprah spends as she sees fit is because she has often stated that money doesn't define her, insisting she would be the same person inside whether she was a celebrity or a fourth-grade teacher like Mrs. Duncan. It is this certainty about herself that has allowed Oprah to keep her equilibrium as her fame and fortune have grown. And of course, she has always tried to make sure that she shares her wealth with those less fortunate, in keeping with her credo, "to whom much is given, much is expected."

When asked in an interview if she had any role models for her philanthropy, she recalled one particular

Christmas in Milwaukee when her mother told her that she simply did not have the money to buy any presents for her children. Oprah was distraught. She knew that after Christmas, all her friends would get together and compare their gifts, and she was humiliated that she would have nothing to show or talk about. Then on Christmas Eve, there was a knock at the door. Several nuns from a nearby church had arrived with a turkey, a fruit basket, and small gifts for Oprah and her brother and sister. She recalls, "I felt such a sense of relief that I would no longer have to be embarrassed when I returned to school. I remember feeling that I mattered enough to these nuns—who I had never met and to this day still don't know their names—and what it meant that they had remembered me."

It is the memory of the nuns' generosity that inspired Oprah to perform a Christmas miracle of her own in 2002. She called it ChristmasKindness, and it took her to South Africa. The trip, in conjunction with the Nelson Mandela Foundation, included visits to orphanages and rural schools in South Africa, and over the course of several weeks, fifty thousand children received gifts of food, clothing, shoes, school supplies, books, and toys.

In the show that Oprah did about her Christmas experience, she introduced viewers to the terrible poverty of South Africa and the horror that AIDS has wreaked on the country. Even a woman as rich as Oprah cannot solve all the problems of a country as poor as South Africa, but she wanted to make a dent. Oprah decided that for her South African initiative, she would bring small gifts of happiness and a large gift of hope.

Because AIDS has killed so many people, South Africa is now a country of orphans—more than one million of them. Throughout sub-Saharan Africa, where a high percentage of the world's orphans live, the figures are even more staggering. In countries like Zambia, Tanzania, and Swaziland, more than eleven million children under the age of fifteen have lost at least one parent to AIDS. In South Africa, sometimes these children are taken in by relatives; others live in the country's few orphanages. Some parentless children simply roam the streets and live as best they can, scrounging for food.

The purpose of Oprah's ChristmasKindness program was to show the children of South Africa that there were people who cared about them, and to bring some pleasure to their lives at holiday time. It took one hundred people and five months to organize the trip. Oprah and her staff personally picked out the jeans, sporting goods, backpacks, radios, and toys that would be given out to the children as Christmas presents. Oprah was particularly insistent that the girls would receive black dolls, something most of them had never seen.

The journey throughout two provinces of South Africa took two weeks and covered hundreds of miles in some of the most inhospitable parts of the country. Twelve times the group raised its huge white tent that was a beacon for children who came from every direction, clapping and singing. Some came in organized groups, others walked alone—some in torn, tattered shoes, some in no shoes in all.

All the children knew was that they had been invited to a party. Sometimes there was traditional dancing, and at several stops, South Africa's beloved former president Nelson Mandela joined the celebration. Also among Oprah's entourage were doctors who were able to treat the children who had medical problems. The high point for the thousands of children attending the parties came when Oprah would announce that each child was getting a back-pack filled with gifts and a brand-new pair of sneakers. The expressions on their young faces were something to behold. Awe, surprise, and joy mingled, as though they could hardly believe their luck. As Oprah com-

On December 8, 2002, Oprah Winfrey visited Durban, South Africa, as part of her ChristmasKindness initiative.

mented, "their energy and joy were contagious." Some of the most moving moments came as the children left their Christmas parties wearing their backpacks, their arms around each other, smiles wide, and eyes bright.

Most of the moments brought almost as much joy to Oprah's group as they did to the children, but there were some frightening incidents as well. At one stop, a windstorm blew up out of nowhere, collapsing one of the huge white tents and trapping some people inside. Others were hit by flying objects that the wind whipped along. Luckily, most of the children had gone home by the time the black clouds blew into the party site; otherwise, things might have been much worse.

Oprah had wanted the children to have one day to know they were appreciated and loved, but she also understood that in order to make any lasting changes, she would have to provide more than candy and sneakers. Toward that end, she decided to start with her long-held belief that education is a window to the world. On her trip to South Africa, with Nelson Mandela by her side, Oprah broke ground for the

Oprah Winfrey Leadership Academy for Girls in Guateng province on December 6, 2002.

The goals of the school are to train the girls to become future leaders of South Africa and to help them fulfill their potential. The teachers were to be chosen from among the best South Africa has to offer. Through the advanced telecommunications system, Oprah would be able to do some teaching from Chicago. Conceived as a boarding school, it would eventually be home to 450 girls who have exhibited academic and leadership skills. The project is funded by Oprah's private foundation.

Despite the hardships and poverty in which the future graduates of her academy had lived, Oprah firmly believes that these girls have the possibility to change their lives. This hope goes back to one of Oprah's core beliefs and one that was articulated in one of her editorials in O magazine: "You become what you believe—not what you wish or want but what you truly believe." Oprah felt that if her academy could give these girls an education and instill in them the belief that they could lead their nation, that is what would eventually happen.

And why not? It is what happened to her. The life of Oprah Winfrey is truly an American success story. From the humblest of beginnings, she has risen to the heights of what this country has to offer, and not only in terms of fame and fortune. She exemplifies America's can-do spirit and the best of its humanitarian impulses.

Several times during her long broadcasting career, she has flirted with the idea of giving up her television show. She was almost sure she was going to retire her show after the 2006 season, but in 2004, she extended her contract until 2011, saying, "The thought of taking the show to its twenty-fifth anniversary is both exhilarating and challenging."

In a DVD Oprah released for her twentieth anniversary, she discussed a music video she'd made as the opening for *The Oprah Winfrey Show*'s 1996–1997 season. In retrospect, she said she had no business singing on a music video, because she wasn't a very good singer. Actually, she wasn't too bad. But what is of most interest is the song she chose to sing. Titled "Run On", it is based on an African American spiritual, and the lyrics speak of learning and love and glories and dreams. The words that seem to encapsulate Oprah's attitude about the future and her hope that the audience will continue to join her as she inspires and encourages people to transform their lives. As the song ends, she offers a simple invitation: "Run with me."

Source Notes

FOREWORD:

"The happiness you . . .": Winfrey, "The Best of Oprah's," 7(originally published in O magazine, May–June 2000).

INTRODUCTION

"I came off . . .": Winfrey, *The Oprah Winfrey Show 20th Anniversary Collection*, Disc 1.

CHAPTER ONE

"Pay attention now . . .": Winfrey, "The Best of Oprah's," 9 (originally published in O magazine, September 2000).

"the result of . . .": Winfrey, "The Best of Oprah's," 30 (originally published in O magazine, July 2001).

"Send clothes.": King, *Everybody Loves Oprah!*, 30.

"I never believed . . .": Winfrey, "The Best of Oprah's," 9 (originally published in O magazine, September 2000).

"I never had . . .": King, *Everybody Loves Oprah!*, 32.

"I wanted to leave . . .": Lee, "When I Was 30."

"My grandmother taught . . ." and "Little Miss Winfrey . . .": Winfrey, interview by Jane Pauley.

"Jesus rose on Easter day . . ." and "Hattie Mae, that girl . . .": Winfrey, "America's Beloved Best Friend," interview by Academy of Achievement.

"She could whip . . .": Adler, ed., *The Uncommon Wisdom*, 8.

"Some of my most . . .": Walker, *Andre Talks Hair*, 11.

"Honey . . ." and "Despite my age . . .": Rubinstein, "Oprah! Thriving on Faith," 140.

"I am where . . ." and "Despite my age . . .": Waldron, *Oprah!*, 11.

CHAPTER TWO

"You'd find a whole . . ." and "I would name them . . .": Rautbord, "Oprah Winfrey," 62.

"You're nothing but . . .": Johnson and Fineman, "Oprah Winfrey," 62.

"I didn't even . . .": Winfrey, "America's Beloved Best Friend," interview by Academy of Achievement.

"'I'm going to fly' . . .": Lee, "When I Was 30."

"Dear Miss Newe . . ." and "What I couldn't . . .": Winfrey, "The Best of Oprah's," 10 (originally published in *O* magazine, September 2000).

"I wanted a father . . .": Waldron, *Oprah!*, 19.

"I owe a lot . . .": Nicholson, *Oprah Winfrey*, 27.

"One of the defining . . .": Winfrey, "A Visit from My Fourth-Grade Teacher (1989)."

"I hadn't seen . . ." "Was I your favorite?" "Why of course . . ." and "You're as pretty . . .": Winfrey, *The Oprah Winfrey Show 20th Anniversary Collection*, Disc 2.

"champion speaker": Nicholson, *Oprah Winfrey*, 27.

"I believed I . . ." "The kids used . . ." "I was an orator . . ." "Out of the night . . ." "Whew, that child . . ." "Whatever you do . . ." "I would listen . . ." and "I was inspired": Winfrey, "America's Beloved Best Friend," interview by Academy of Achievement.

"I wrote them . . ." "Here comes that . . ." and "I don't care . . .": Winfrey, "The Best of Oprah's," 5 (originally published in O magazine, May–June 2000).

"We had brought . . .": Mair, Oprah Winfrey, 14.

CHAPTER THREE

"I first learned . . .": Winfrey, "The Best of Oprah's," 61 (originally published in O magazine, November 2002).

"It happened over . . . ,": Barthel, "Oprah," 56.

"Born at the Right Time": Winfrey, "The Best of Oprah's," 45 (originally published in O magazine, February 2002).

"The life I . . ." Mair, Oprah Winfrey, 17.

"her way of showing . . .": Lowe, Oprah Winfrey Speaks, 10.

"I caused all . . .": Adler, The Uncommon Wisdom, 16.

"I felt so bad . . ." Krohn, Oprah Winfrey, 28

The dialogue between Oprah and her mother was recounted by Oprah Winfrey on the Late Show with David Letterman, December 1, 2005, and the incident noted in almost every source.

I'm a smart girl . . . : Friedrich, Oprah Winfrey, 21.

CHAPTER FOUR

"take to [her] bed . . ." and "I hid my . . .": Randolph, "Oprah Opens Up," 5.

"in shame . . .": Randolph, "Oprah Opens Up," 4.

"honored me by taking . . .": Randolph, "Oprah Opens Up," 5.

"My father's discipline . . .": King, Everybody Loves Oprah!, 58.

"If I tell you . . .": Waldron, *Oprah!*, 42–43.

"If you were . . .": Culhane, "Oprah Winfrey," 103.

"I had a tree . . ." and "Well, first of all . . .": Winfrey, "America's Beloved Best Friend."

"It was the first . . .": Winfrey, "Oprah's Cut with Maya Angelou."

"We knew she . . .": Friedrich, *Oprah Winfrey*, 28.

"She could just about . . .": Ryan, "Uprising at the Church of Oprah."

"She had these . . .": Mair, *Oprah Winfrey*, 26.

"Regarding your question . . .": Mair, *Oprah Winfrey*, 25.

"I got a feeling . . ." and "The green grass . . .": Mair, *Oprah Winfrey*, 28.

"One thing I remember . . ." and "We gotta talk.": Mair, *Oprah Winfrey*, 31.

WVOL information comes from Winfrey, "The Man Who Discovered Oprah."

CHAPTER FIVE

Description of Miss Fire Safety Contest: Winfrey, "America's Beloved Best Friend."

"I hated . . ." and "It was in . . .": Friedrich, *Oprah Winfrey*, 33.

"Don't you know . . ." King, *Everybody Loves Oprah!*, 78.

"You try to have . . .": King, *Everybody Loves Oprah!*, 79.

"It was unbelievable . . .": Friedrich, *Oprah Winfrey*, 39.

"It was a very racially . . .": Friedrich, *Oprah Winfrey*, 41.

"We don't shake . . .": Waldron, *Oprah!*, 84.

"happy, paid token . . . ": Friedrich, *Oprah Winfrey*, 41.

"Until you do . . .": Winfrey, "The Best of Oprah's," 31 (originally published in *O* magazine, July 2001).

"I was devastated . . .": Winfrey, "America's Beloved Best Friend."

"Your hair's too . . .": King, *Everybody Loves Oprah!*, 89.

"chi-chi, pooh-pooh salon . . .": King, *Everybody Loves Oprah!*, 90.

"In a week I . . .": King, *Everybody Loves Oprah!*, 91.

"I went through . . .": King, *Everybody Loves Oprah!*, 92.

"They tried to convince . . .": Winfrey, "America's Beloved Best Friend."

"luck is preparation . . ." and "I said to myself . . .": Lowe, *Oprah Winfrey Speaks*, 79.

"was a universal woman . . .": Mair, *Oprah Winfrey*, 48.

"Then, one night . . ." "And with the exception . . ." "One day I . . ." and "You should go . . .": Winfrey, "The Best of Oprah's," 34 (originally published in O magazine, August 2002).

CHAPTER SIX

"How do you . . ." "I think it . . ." "You know, I'm . . ." "I'm looking at . . ." "And you know . . ." "And so have . . . ." "What's that?" "Your head fits . . ." "Do you really . . ." and "I do": Krohn, *Oprah Winfrey*, 56.

"Just walking down . . ." *The Oprah Winfrey 20th Anniversary Collection.* Disc 1.

Roger Ebert incident: Ebert, "How I Gave Oprah Her Start."

"Talk-show hosts . . .": Mr Showbiz.com, June 2003.

"My ability . . .": Winfrey, "America's Beloved Best Friend."

"Thus began . . .": Winfrey, "The Best of Oprah's," 53 (originally published in O magazine, August 2002).

Tonight Show incident: King, *Everybody Loves Oprah!*, 130–31.

"I prayed, 'Lord . . .'": *The Oprah Winfrey Show 20th Anniversary Collection*, Disc 1

Description of Spielberg's call: *The Oprah Winfrey Show*, December 9, 2005.

CHAPTER SEVEN

"This morning I sat . . .": Winfrey, "Broadway Dreams."

"I was surprised . . ." and "that's what the book . . .": Mathews, "3 'Color Purple' Actresses Talk about Its Impact," in *Los Angeles Times*.

"Perhaps God was . . .": Rubinstein, "Oprah! Thriving on Faith."

"She travels . . .": King, "Interview with Stedman Graham."

"You want something . . .": Adler, *The Uncommon Wisdom*, 21.

"We laugh . . ." "She has helped . . ." and "For every new . . .": Winfrey, "The Best of Oprah's," 34 (originally published in O magazine, August 2001).

"I keep wondering . . .": Winfrey, *The Oprah Winfrey Show 20th Anniversary Collection*, Disc 1.

Forsyth County show and AIDS show discussion: Winfrey, *The Oprah Winfrey Show 20th Anniversary Collection*, Disc 4.

"I was the one . . .": Winfrey, *The Oprah Winfrey Show 20th Anniversary Collection*, Disc 1.

"Had I not . . .": Mair, *Oprah Winfrey*, 133.

"This is really . . .": Mair, *Oprah Winfrey*, 134.

"a sudden, soaring success" "I communicate . . ." and "I think we . . .": *60 Minutes*, December 14, 1986.

CHAPTER EIGHT

"I was the smallest . . ." "so I put the syrup . . ." and the discussion of Oprah's weight: Winfrey, *The Oprah Winfrey Show 20th Anniversary Collection*, Disc 4.

"There are days . . .": King, *Everybody Loves Oprah!*, 179.

Stedman incident: Randolph, "Oprah Opens Up."

"mortified" "waddle" "I felt like . . ." and "I gotta eat . . .": Powell, "I Was Trying to Fill Something Deeper."

"'I'm Oprah Winfrey . . .'" and "I would ask Bob . . .": Winfrey, *The Oprah Winfrey Show 20th Anniversary Collection*, Disc 5.

"Girl, no need . . ." and "undermined all my . . .": Winfrey, "The Best of Oprah's," 11 (originally published in O magazine, September 2000).

"My family . . .": Friedrich, *Oprah Winfrey*, 67.

"The experience . . . .": Friedrich, *Oprah Winfrey*, 25.

"I went home . . ." and "You don't deserve . . .": Randolph, "Oprah Opens Up," 4.

"I should have . . ." "a masterful job" and "I wanted to . . .": Randolph, "Oprah Opens Up," 2.

CHAPTER NINE

"I've been guilty . . .": Friedrich, *Oprah Winfrey*, 80.

"I want to use . . .": Ryan, "Uprising at the Church of Oprah."

"We've grown in the past . . .": Lowe, *Oprah Winfrey Speaks*, 150.

"So it happened . . ." and "I would . . . speak . . .": Winfrey, "America's Beloved Best Friend."

"Almost does not . . .": Friedrich, *Oprah Winfrey*, 73.

"I'm Oprah Winfrey . . .": *Scared Silent: Exposing Child Abuse*, 1992.

"Enough is enough . . .": *The Oprah Winfrey Show*, October 6, 2005.

"He just stopped me cold . . .": Lawrence, *The World According to Oprah*, 130.

"carefully and maliciously . . .": Friedrich, *Oprah Winfrey*, 85.

"the things that happen . . ." and "Everyone has a trial . . .": Winfrey, *The Oprah Winfrey Show 20th Anniversary Collection*, Disc 4.

"Free speech not . . .": Lawrence, *The World According to Oprah*, 131.

"the world's largest . . .": Winfrey, "The Small Change Campaign."

CHAPTER TEN

"We might be poor . . .": Mair, *Oprah Winfrey*, 283.

"It was the greatest . . .": Winfrey, "Oprah's Favorite Books Gallery."

"It's a love story . . ." and "I wanted to connect . . .": BBC News Online, "Oprah Winfrey and Beloved."

"I became hysterical . . .": Krohn, *Oprah Winfrey*, 91.

"ruined, overwhelmed, and redeemed . . .": Randolph, "Oprah Opens Up," 4.

"Today I'm doing this . . .": Krohn, *Oprah Winfrey*, 91.

"To create a movie . . ." "Well, you did that . . ." "In that moment . . ." and "to do your best . . .": Winfrey, "The Best of Oprah's," 21 (originally published in O magazine, February 2001).

"Why don't we . . .": Winfrey, *The Oprah Winfrey Show 20th Anniversary Collection*, Disc 5.

"the underlying message . . .": *Larry King Live*, January 12, 2006.

"I made a mistake . . .": *The Oprah Winfrey Show*, January 26, 2006.

"What I like . . ." and "O reflects the . . .": "Oprah Winfrey Magazine Named."

"I know to you guys . . .": Krohn, *Oprah Winfrey*, 99.

"There's an energy . . .": Winfrey, "Broadway Dreams," 2.

CHAPTER ELEVEN

"out of sorts" "injected . . ." "If he could . . ." "We walked in . . ."

and description of Oprah's fiftieth birthday party: Winfrey, *The Oprah Winfrey Show 20th Anniversary Collection*, Disc 6.

"I felt such a . . .": *Late Show with David Letterman*, December 1, 2005.

"their energy and joy . . ." and the description of Christmas Kindness in South Africa: Winfrey, *The Oprah Winfrey Show 20th Anniversary Collection*, Disc 6.

"You become what . . .": Winfrey, "The Best of Oprah's," 9 (originally published in O magazine, September 2000).

"The thought of . . .": Hollywood.com, Harpo press release.

"Run with me": Winfrey, "Vintage Oprah."

Bibliography

Adler, Bill, ed. *The Uncommon Wisdom of Oprah Winfrey: A Portrait in Her Own Words*. Secaucus, N.J.: Birch Lane Press, 1997.

Allen, Jenny. "Oprah Winfrey." *Us Weekly*, June 12, 2000.

Barthel, Joan. "Oprah." *Ms.* magazine, August 1986, 56.

BBC News Online. "Oprah Winfrey and Beloved," March 5, 1999. http://news.bbc.co.uk/1/hi/entertainment/290601.stm.

Culhane, John. "Oprah Winfrey: How the Truth Changed Her Life." *Reader's Digest*, February 1989.

Ebert, Roger. "How I Gave Oprah Her Start." http://rogerebert.suntimes.com/apps/pbcs.d11/article?AID=/20051116/COMMENTARY/511160301 (p. 8).

Edwards, Audrey. "The O Factor." *Essence* magazine, October 3, 2003.

Friedrich, Belinda. *Oprah Winfrey*. Women of Achievement. New York: Chelsea House, 2001.

Johnson, Marilyn, and Dana Fineman. "Oprah Winfrey: A Life in Books," *LIFE* magazine, September 1997.

King, Larry. "Interview with Stedman Graham." *Larry King Live*, October 3, 2003. http://transcripts.cnn.com/TRANSCRIPTS/0310/03/lkl.00.htm.

King, Norman. *Everybody Loves Oprah!: Her Remarkable Life Story.* New York: William Morrow & Co., 1987.

Krohn, Katherine. *Oprah Winfrey.* Minneapolis: Lerner Publications, 2002.

Lawrence, Ken. *The World According to Oprah: An Unauthorized Portrait in Her Own Words.* New York: Andrews McMeel Publishing, 2005

Lee, Vernita. "When I was 30: Vernita Lee." Interview by Nicole Sweeney. *mkeonline*, May 19, 2005. http://www.mkeonline.com/story.asp?id=326705.

Lowe, Janet. *Oprah Winfrey Speaks: Insight from the World's Most Influential Voice.* New York: John Wiley & Sons, 1998.

Mair, George. *Oprah Winfrey: The Real Story.* New York: Birch Lane Press, 1994.

Mathews, Jack. "3 'Color Purple' Actresses Talk about Its Impact." *Los Angeles Times*, January 31, 1986.

Mr Showbiz.com. http://www.mrshowbiz.go.com/people/oprah-winfrey/content/bio.html. June 2003.

Nicholson, Lois P. *Oprah Winfrey*. Black Americans of Achievement. New York: Chelsea House, 1994.

"Oprah Winfrey Magazine Named: O, the Oprah Magazine." The Write News, January 12, 2000. http://www.writenews.com/2000/011200_o_oprah.htm.

Powell, Joanna. "I Was Trying to Fill Something Deeper." *Good Housekeeping*, October 1996.

Randolph, Laura B. "Oprah Opens Up About Her Weight, Her Wedding and Why She Withheld the Book." *Ebony* magazine, October 1993.

Rautbord, Sugar. "Oprah Winfrey." *Interview* magazine, March 1986, 62.

Rubinstein, Leslie. "Oprah! Thriving on Faith." *McCall's*, August 1987.

Ryan, Joal. "Uprising at the Church of Oprah." *Eonline*, October 17, 1998. http://www.eonline.com/News/Items/0,1,3763,00.html.

Taylor, LaTonya. "The Church of O." *Christianity Today*, April 1, 2002.

Waldron, Robert. *Oprah!* New York: St. Martin's Press, 1987.

Walker, Andre. *Andre Talks Hair*. New York: Simon & Schuster, 1997.

Westen, Robin. *Oprah Winfrey: "I Don't Believe in Failure."* African-American Biography Library. New York: Enslow, 2005.

Winfrey, Oprah. "America's Beloved Best Friend." Interview by Academy of Achievement. February 21, 1991.

Winfrey, Oprah. "The Best of Oprah's 'What I Know for Sure.'" *O* magazine, May 2005.

Winfrey Oprah. "Broadway Dreams." http://www2.oprah.com/presents/2005/purple/slide/20051111/purple_20051111_350_301.jhtml.

Winfrey, Oprah. Interview by Jane Pauley. *Real Life with Jane Pauley*. NBC, September 6, 1991.

Winfrey, Oprah. "The Man Who Discovered Oprah." http://www.oprah.com/pastshows/200401/tows_past_20040127.jhtml.

Winfrey, Oprah. "Oprah's Favorite Books Gallery." http://www.oprah.com/books/favorite/books_favorite_main.jhtml.

Winfrey, Oprah. "Oprah's Cut with Maya Angelou." http://www.oprah.com/omagazine/200012/omag_200012_maya.jhtml.

Winfrey, Oprah. *The Oprah Winfrey Show 20th Anniversary Collection* DVD set. Hollywood, CA: Paramount Home Video, 2005.

Winfrey, Oprah. "The Small Change Campaign (1997)." http://www.oprah.com/presents/2005/20anniv/oprah/oprah_moments_284_108.jhtml.

Winfrey, Oprah. "Vintage Oprah: Lyrics to *The Oprah Winfrey Show* Theme Songs. http://www.oprah.com/tows/vintage/past/vintage_past_lyrics.jhtml#butch

Winfrey, Oprah. "A Visit from My Fourth-Grade Teacher (1989)." http://www.oprah.com/presents/2005/20anniv/oprah/oprah_moments_284_103.jhtml.

60 Minutes. December 14, 1986.

Larry King Live. October 3, 2003.

Larry King Live. January 12, 2006.

Late Show with David Letterman. December 1, 2005.

The Oprah Winfrey Show. December 9, 2005.

The Oprah Winfrey Show. January 26, 2006.

Scared Silent: Exposing Child Abuse. September 4, 1992.

Index

Photo Credits